PROFITABLE CUSTOMERS

ACKNOWLEDGEMENTS

Customer Base Management has evolved during numerous consulting projects. I am indebted to the thousands of sales, service and marketing staff as well as the managers and directors who have been involved in these assignments. This book has also depended upon the 473 companies which have taken the time to respond to surveys conducted by Abberton Associates. Customer Base Management has also relied upon the support from the team at Abberton Associates. In addition, Peter McLaren, Michael Coire, Charlotte Gosling, James Bennett, Warren Chester and Don McQueen have all contributed to the development of the thinking. My thanks also go to OC&C Strategy Consultants for awakening the interest in customer base issues and developing some of the analytical frameworks which appear in this book. However, I am most indebted to John Wilson and Helen Barker for the hard work, support and encouragement they have provided during the past five years. Most of all I thank Rowena for her patience and understanding which have proved invaluable in completing this project.

PROFESSIONAL
PAPERBACKS

PROFITABLE CUSTOMERS

HOW TO IDENTIFY, DEVELOP AND RETAIN THEM

SECOND EDITION

Charles Wilson

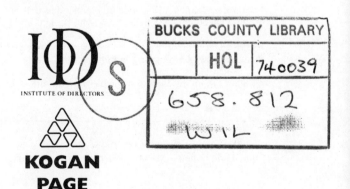

INSTITUTE OF DIRECTORS

KOGAN
PAGE

LONDON, UK • NEW HAMPSHIRE, USA • NEW DELHI, INDIA

YOURS TO HAVE AND TO HOLD

BUT NOT TO COPY

First published in 1996
Second edition printed in paperback 1998

Kogan Page Limited
120 Pentonville Road
London N1 9JN

The Institute of Directors accepts no responsibility for the opinions expressed by the author of this publication. Readers should consult their advisors before acting on any of the issues raised.

British Library Cataloguing in Publication Data

A CIP record for this book is available from the British Library.

ISBN 0 7494 2825 2

Typeset by Saxon Graphics Ltd, Derby
Printed and bound in Great Britain by Biddles Ltd, Guildford and King's Lynn.

Contents

PREFACE

The inspiration for customer base management dates back to 1991. I had spent the late 1980s and early 1990s consulting to various 'blue chips' who were re-organizing their selling and marketing operations. In 1991 this experience was summarized in a report entitled *Balancing the Salesforce Equation* which won acclaim and invitations to several prospective clients. One prospect, a medium sized UK Plc, invited me to their three day strategy workshop. At the end of this intensive session several thoughts struck home:

- Virtually all the time was spent discussing internal issues, new products, new markets, re-designing the business process and undertaking a SWOT analysis. In all this time nobody mentioned how trade channels were restructuring, how customer purchasing behaviour was changing or the fact that the top 10 per cent of customers accounted for over 65 per cent of sales and virtually all the company's profits. Trade channel management and customer development had 'slipped the agenda', yet it was a critical factor in determining corporate success.
- Sales, service R&D and marketing departments were poorly co-ordinated. This resulted in inefficiency and poor customer service. It later emerged that the supplier could cut its interface costs by 35 per cent whilst improving customer development and retention.
- When customer service was mentioned it tended to be in the form of dangerous clichés such as 'the customer is king'. There was a lot of 'lip service' paid to the customer: however this did not translate into profitable, tangible action.
- The firm's profit and loss systems measured the profitability of products and divisions, but nobody knew the true profitability of different customers. After examination it emerged that the profit margin obtained from different customers deviated far more than the margin from alternative products.

Following conversations with other clients and consultants, it became apparent that these problems were common across a broad variety of industry sectors and companies. In 1994 Abberton Associates conducted a survey of over 200 firms which endorsed the initial observations. The survey was entitled *Customer Base Control* which highlighted common failings and opportunities to improve the management of the customer base. In 1997 this survey was updated. This book has developed the original findings to focus on how customer base management can be used to build sales, improve margins and reduce the costs of interfacing with the customers. It is intended for those CEOs and Sales/Marketing/Customer Service/Finance managers who are committed to improving profits through effective customer base management.

INTRODUCTION

Three simultaneous phone calls – which one do you take?

Line 1: An angry customer who is dissatisfied with the service your firm is providing.

Line 2: A big, potential customer.

Line 3: A major shareholder.

You have probably been told that 'the customer is king' so many times that your first instinct is to soothe the customer on Line 1. But is this really your best strategy? What if the customer is small and unprofitable? Should you risk losing a big potential customer because you spend time and resources on one who is contributing nothing to your bottom line?

This highlights a fundamental management issue. How does your firm deploy its resources relative to the customer base? How do you ensure that marketing, sales and service staff are deployed to maximize long-term profits? The majority of management teams ignore this crucial question and leave sales and customer service staff to determine which customers will receive what attention. Such an approach is risky. Sloppy management of the customer base results in lost sales, poor margins and a high cost of serving the customer. Customers were not created equal and warrant different levels of service. In fact, when all the costs of serving a customer are properly allocated, a supplier can usually find that between 30 and 50 per cent of customers are unprofitable. Meanwhile, suppliers are increasingly dependent on a smaller group of customers for the majority of profits. As these customers grow bigger and more sophisticated they tend to demand better service and lower prices. Herein lies the problem for the supplier. How can it respond effectively to the needs of profitable customers if its resources are being deployed serving those which will never produce a profit?

To compound the issue, there is enormous change at the buyer/customer interface. New ways of working are having a profound impact on the way customers and suppliers inter-relate. Some customers are seeking a lasting partnership with suppliers while others are happy with a cheap night out. Some require automated linkages while others still want face-to-face contact. Moreover, new technology is redefining the way suppliers and customers can interrelate. The computer allows suppliers to obtain a far more detailed understanding of the needs of customer groups and individual buyers. Technology also allows new suppliers with better customer management systems to enter the market. These operators employ the latest systems to reach the most profitable customers within a market. Companies like Dell computers, Direct Line Insurance and First Direct bank have employed the telephone and Internet to 'cherry pick' the most attractive customers within their respective markets, leaving conventional suppliers to scramble to defend profits. Take as an example Direct Line Insurance in the UK. In 1985 it recognized that conventional auto insurers were incurring high costs because they were using agents and sales representatives to sell the service. By selling over the telephone, Direct Line was able to save this expense while obtaining a more detailed understanding of customer requirements. It was better able to forecast the liabilities associated with different drivers and could price accordingly. Direct Line undercut traditional operators while providing superior customer service. The combination of lower costs and better service proved formidable. Direct Line quickly grew to dominate the auto insurance market leaving traditional insurers to adopt the same business system or quit the market.

Just as Direct Line has used the telephone and computer to revolutionize the way motor insurance is sold, the technology of the future will spawn a new generation of suppliers which offer better service at a lower cost. These operators will be able to 'cherry pick' the most attractive customers within a market which will have a devastating impact on conventional supplier/customer relationships.

Despite these risks and challenges, most suppliers undermanage their customer base. They fail to understand where the profit opportunities reside within their customer base and often provide an average service at high cost. Such firms can still be addressing an illusory 'market' while their smarter competitors manage the specific needs and profitability of small customer groups or individual customers.

This book is designed to help suppliers manage the customer base more effectively. It reviews the opportunities to build sales, defend margins and minimize the cost of interfacing with the customer. It considers the ways to identify profitable and unprofitable customers. It then explores the routes by which profitable customers can be locked-in and developed. Lock-ins include strengthening the bond with customers, developing 'handcuffs' and building loyalty. The supplier can then work to build income by increasing purchase frequency, raising average transaction values and going deeper into the 'customer's pocket'.

Having locked in the core customers, the supplier can tighten the costs of interfacing with the customer by harnessing new technology or formulating new ways of serving customers. The supplier can then overhaul the management of the customer lifecycle, ie manage the customer through its recruitment, development and decline.

To improve the management of the customer base, the supplier might need to make changes to the firm's culture, organization, remuneration or approach. It might need to junk obsolete trade channels, reject outdated pricing structures, or scrap inappropriate systems. Such changes might be difficult but they allow the supplier to guarantee that its resources are deployed where they will have the maximum impact on customer service and long-term profitability.

THE CUSTOMER BASE 'PROFIT GAP' IS WIDENING

When a supplier formally reviews the income it receives from each account and then apportions the true costs of serving that customer, it will probably get a shock. It is likely to find that a core group of customers account for a disproportionately large slice of profits. For example:

- a European speciality retailer discovered that 52 per cent of its sales and virtually all its profits were obtained from 10 per cent of customers;

- a US bank realized that 17 per cent of customers produced all the profits;

- a British speciality chemicals firm produced 50 per cent of profits from just 2 per cent of customers.

The supplier would receive a bigger shock if it compared the profitability of the customer base today with that of a decade ago. Profits within the customer base have shifted, and a typically smaller percentage of customers now account for a larger share of profits. There is nothing wrong in being dependent upon a few, large customers. However, there is serious danger if your firm is highly dependent upon a small group of customers which it has not identified. The common assumption is that the biggest customers are the biggest earners, but this is not necessarily the case. For example, when a major European printing equipment manufacturer reviewed its customer base profitability, it transpired that the profits were not where they were expected to be. Worse still it had failed to recognize that the profits had shifted significantly within the customer base since the early 1980s. In the early 1980s, virtually all customers contributed to the bottom line. Margins were strong and the majority of customers bought the product 'off the shelf'. By 1992 the position had changed. Big customers had grown quickly and demanded better margins. They also required the product to be tailored to their specific needs. Key account managers and special teams were appointed to support these accounts. Meanwhile, a higher proportion of R&D time was dedicated to their needs. Thus the costs of selling and serving the customer increased as a proportion of the manufacturing price. The result was a profound shift in the profitability of different sorts of customers. As Figure 2.2 shows, the top 10 per cent of customers switched from producing 15 per cent of company profits to being unprofitable. Meanwhile, the supplier was milking 29 per cent of its profits from the third decile of customers.

Big turned out not to be beautiful and the milking of medium sized customers turned sour. A competitor recognized the profitability of 'middle sized' companies and started to aggressively target them with better service. Too much of the supplier's resources were tied up in over serving unprofitable customers so it could not respond quickly enough to lock in the profitable customer. The supplier lost share in the most profitable part of the market and company profits collapsed.

This situation is not unique. In fact, when the same exercise was conducted by a UK retailer, an equipment manufacturer, an outsourcing agency and a chemicals company, the same pattern emerged (see Figure 2.1). In each case profitability had shifted within the customer base and the supplier had become more dependent on its top five per cent of customers. Fortunately, in these later cases the supplier recognized the issue before it was exploited by a competitor.

It is worth examining the factors which are shifting profit within the customer base. Typically the supplier is confronted by five issues:

▨ customers are more powerful;

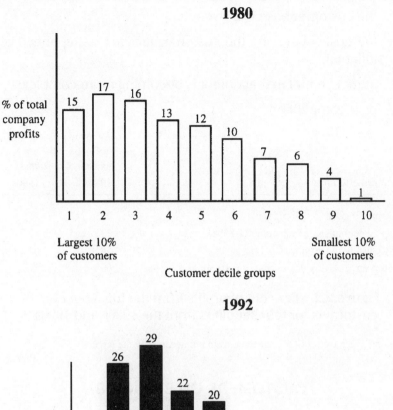

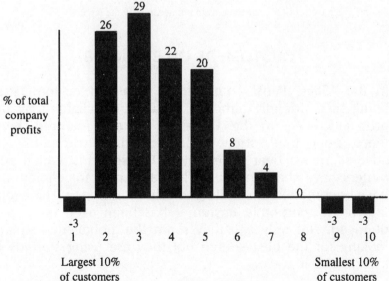

Figure 2.1   The widening rift between profitable and unprofitable customers: the per cent of company profit by customer decile (each decile = 10% of customer base).
Source: Supplier to the European printing industry (turnover £200 million).

▨ the customer base is fragmenting;

▨ the costs of serving the customer are increasing ahead of inflation;

▨ trade channel management is becoming more complex;

▨ new competition.

Company (turnover)	Company per cent of profits from the top 5 per cent of customers	
	1980s	1990s
UK mixed goods retailer (£1bn)	29	38
Capital equipment manufacturer (£0.3bn)	33	42
UK outsourcing agency (£0.1bn)	58	63
European speciality chemicals firm (£0.3bn)	60	77

Figure 2.2 Per cent of profits from the top 5 per cent of customers for four suppliers from the 1980s and 1990s.*

*Note: The most profitable customers are not necessarily the largest

CUSTOMERS ON STEROIDS

In the 1960s, Pepsi commercials depicted customers as being nice, friendly airheads who were delighted by the product's taste. In the 1990s the adverts featured 'been there, done that', streetwise, calculating customers. The advertisements bear testimony to the speed at which customers have sharpened up. They are spoilt for choice and have become experts in finding value for money. The evolution of the corporate customer has been even more pronounced. Not only can they roam the global marketplace looking for the best source but they are using steroids to increase their power.

Spoilt for choice

In the 1930s, denim jeans were manufactured in a handful of countries. Today there are over 40 jeans-producing nations. In

1984 there were five major suppliers of personal computers. Today an American PC buyer can choose from more than fifty firms. Thanks to the globalization, saturation and acceleration of markets, the industrial and domestic buyer has a spectrum of choice that was unimaginable 20 years ago.

Globalization

Changes in GATT, improved communications and the opening up of low wage countries such as China and India are accelerating the pace of globalization. Market dominance in the ship-building industry has passed through three countries in 20 years. In the early 1970s the US was the market leader. Then Japan overtook the US, and now Korea has surpassed Japan. But not for long. Despite the huge capital expenditure involved and the long lead times, ship buyers move quickly to the best value sources. In the next decade China will probably grow to be the world's largest producer of ships.

Even high value-added industries are experiencing globalisation. Look at the computer software industry. In the mid-1990s computer firms discovered that software can be written in India more quickly and at half the price of Silicon Valley. Computer code and programming can be easily passed 'over the wire' between Bangalore and the United States. The Indian staff are often more diligent and faster than their Western counterparts, yet they cost only 15 per cent of their equivalent in Silicon Valley. As a result the Bangalore software industry has grown to more than a billion dollars in less than a decade.

As communication costs and trade barriers fall and suppliers become more desperate for labour cost savings, many other industries will experience a similar globalisation of production. This allows customers to source them further afield. Millions of British beer drinkers now day-trip to France to buy alcohol at reduced prices and customers in most business-to-business sectors are comparing cross-border prices to obtain the best deal. For example, in the 1950s Burton Menswear (the UK's largest men's clothing retailer) sourced from four countries. Today it sources from over 40. Grey markets in cosmetics, pharmaceuticals and computers bear witness to the harmonization of international prices.

Transnational buying groups exacerbate the problem. Members can compare prices from the same supplier across Europe and can negotiate the lowest rate. Meanwhile, on-line databases allow buyers to compare cross-border prices at the press of a button.

Saturation

The international explosion in trade has been accompanied by enormous expansion in capacity. More companies, more production sites, higher productivity and lower inflation have combined to make a buyers' paradise. A buyer of ignition components in Germany can now choose from 27 suppliers, whereas there were only 8 in 1985. In this buyer's utopia component quality and performance has improved while the real cost has fallen by over 30 per cent in 5 years.

Increased choice can also be seen in consumer markets. In the US, retail square footage has increased fourfold since 1960 while real demand has only doubled. More store capacity and a higher number of major stores provide more opportunities for the customer to find the best offer.

Acceleration

The acceleration of product lifecycles has strengthened the customer's hand. Buyers are able to wait until the optimal time to buy. During the launch of Windows 95, commercial buyers held off upgrading their Windows and DOS systems in the belief that the longer they waited, the better value the Windows 95 upgrade would be. In essence, buyers were using older, 'good enough' versions of Microsoft operating systems to create competition for Windows 95.

The changes in the global marketplace cannot be underestimated. Customers have more choice, which in turn gives them more power. Your organization might be working hard to win customers. But in five years it will be fighting a swarm of new competitors from far-off places with radically different economics. In the global marketplace your business will have to work much harder to keep your current customers and win new ones.

Customer sophistication

Increasing expectations

Customers are becoming accustomed to exceptional levels of service. Dominos will deliver a hot, £5 pizza in 30 minutes. Viking Direct can deliver £30 of discount office supplies to your door within five hours. In every walk of life customers can receive service which would have been deemed incredible a decade ago. In Argentina a grocery shopper can go to three of the world's best retailers: Carrefour (France), Makro (Netherlands) or Walmart (US). They can buy their fast-food at McDonald's or Pizza Hut. It is hardly surprising that the customer expects a similar level of value, courtesy and service from Argentina's department stores and variety retailers. Given this high level of expectation, suppliers are 'benchmarked' against the world's best rather than against direct domestic competitors. Commercial buyers are even more advanced and have developed 'steroids' to enhance their natural advantage.

Better people

In the 1970s the buying function was perceived as a dull backwater which attracted low calibre managers. But in the intervening two decades corporate interest in quality, 'supply chain management' and 'just-in-time' highlighted the need for talent in the buying office. Consequently, the salaries for buyers increased at a faster rate than those of sales people. Better compensation and enhanced status attracted more graduates and higher calibre managers into the procurement office.

New tools

In 1980 supplier appraisal systems, formalized tender procedures, open-book accounting and supplier cost simulation were rare. Today they are widely adopted by smart buyers. Figure 2.3 shows the extent to which such tools are being employed by 'smart' buyers and explains the reasons why they were adopted.

Tools Used	% of Response
Formal tender systems	64
Supplier appraisal systems	72
Open book accounting	18
Supplier cost simulation	12

Reasons for introducing supplier appraisal	% of Response
Improve quality	92%
Reduce costs	71%
Eliminate inspection	64%
Reduce supply base	54%

Figure 2.3　Increasing sophistication of tools used by buyers in the UK.

Source: Abberton Associates survey of 172 UK firms (1997).

This sophistication has caught many suppliers off guard. As Warren E Norquist, Polaroid's Purchasing VP, commented in *Purchasing* magazine:

> Many suppliers know even less about their costs than their customers do . . . We model supplier costs in every detail to understand the cost structure and to avoid price inflation.

The results have been substantial. One purchasing manager for a French engineering manufacturer commented:

> Improved supplier controls have taken two percent from our suppliers and put it straight onto our bottom line.

In the next five years these tools will be even more widespread. The EU already requires that all major public sector projects be put out to tender. Meanwhile finance directors are becoming interested in open-book accounting and cost simulation. This leaves traditional salespeople ill-equipped to deal with these better informed and better armed customers.

Improved systems

Technology is strengthening the buyer's hand. At Debenhams, the UK department store, it used to take days to obtain the basic information to properly monitor supplier performance. Many buyers failed to complete the process because of the time required. Suppliers found they could 'get away with all sorts of tricks'. Subsequently, Debenhams introduced a new merchandising system which allows buyers to appraise supplier performance in a matter of minutes. As CEO, Terry Green, commented:

> When you formally appraise suppliers to produce a ranking, the weak performers become obvious. Either they buck up to meet the standards or they are dropped . . . we have so far dropped over four hundred suppliers and have developed strong relationships with the best suppliers.

Enhanced buying structures

Most customers have refined their buying structures in an attempt to improve the effectiveness of the procurement function. They have centralized decision making at head office and increased buyer specialization. General Motors established a single global purchasing centre to replace its 27 separate buying offices. Centralization increased the average contract size. GM can thereby consolidate volumes to reduce prices. More importantly, centralization allowed buyers to enhance their buying expertise. Rather than having four buyers purchasing ignition systems for their respective countries, a central team can work to understand every aspect of the product. This expertise forces suppliers to reduce total costs.

Another buying structure improvement has been the adoption of 'team buying'. Each member of the team is an expert in one part of the buying decision and ensures that the team gets the best price, service and value. For example, team buying in a hospital might be done by three experts. A nurse specifies the type of bandage, the stock manager identifies the best inventory arrangements and the accountant computes the lowest total price. A team structure works well for customers, but it can be a supplier's nightmare. As a sales executive from ICI Paints commented:

> The buying team is difficult. You don't know who is the decision maker and you are left dealing with a load of experts, all of them with an axe to grind.

Easier to switch

Business relationships are not what they used to be. Customers are finding that it is easier to terminate a supplier relationship without paying a penalty. For example, in the 1970s a house buyer required a long history with a bank before being eligible for a mortgage. Today a buyer can shop between banks to find the lowest-cost mortgage. If the individual has a good credit record (the details of which are stored at a central credit agency such as CCN) they will have little problem obtaining the money. In the computer industry in the 1970s, renters of IBM mainframes tended to do all their business with IBM. A new system would have spoken a different 'language' and switching was too disruptive. Today all computers share a common language so a company can switch from IBM to Compaq to Dell with ease. Likewise, in the 1970s a German haulier with a Mercedes fleet would always buy from that supplier. The haulier had an inventory of Mercedes spare parts and could not afford to carry a parallel inventory. Today the inventory required for a fleet is minimal because there are fewer breakdowns and the parts can be easily obtained.

In the past a customer would find it difficult to switch from one supplier to another without paying a penalty. Higher interest rates, a new computer platform, a new inventory of parts or additional staff training to handle a new product were all common barriers. Today a customer can switch from AT&T to MCI by speaking to a sales person on a phone, or a new Visa card can be opened in a matter of seconds and a mortgage can be awarded over the telephone. The customer can now easily switch from one supplier to another without incurring a penalty.

Margin pressure

Bigger, smarter, stronger customers tend to do a better job of extracting value from suppliers. This often depresses the suppliers' margins. US clothing shoppers bear testimony to this trend. Their enthusiasm to find the best value fostered the growth of discounters such as Walmart, TJ Maxx and Marshalls where you 'never, never, never pay full price'. The discount sector now accounts for around 35 per cent of US clothing sales. These operators are accustomed to working on gross margins which are half of those expected by a regular clothing retailer.

Manufacturers are experiencing the same pressures. Whilst at General Motors' José Ignacio Lopez de Arriortùa and his buying 'warriors' put approximately $4 billion onto the 1993 bottom line through aggressive supplier cost control and the reviewing of supplier contracts. Dr Lopez and many of the warriors subsequently moved to Volkswagen and further refined their procurement strategies. They offered suppliers such as SIV, Europe's second largest windscreen manufacturer, larger contracts if SIV lowered their prices by 15 per cent and reduced costs by 3 per cent per annum for several years thereafter.

Other corporations are employing similar initiatives. In 1992 General Electric Co introduced 'Target 10'. Suppliers were gathered together and told that they had to cut their unit costs by 10 per cent and continue to reduce costs thereafter. As one supplier commented:

> It was a body-blow. We were already at the bone and they wanted 10% more.

Similarly, in October 1995 Ford announced that suppliers would be required to freeze their prices until the end of the century. Suppliers would bear any inflation or product upgrade costs. Ford spends around £37 billion on parts. So by imposing the cost freeze it should produce savings worth around £8 billion by 2000. Unless suppliers can recover the profits through increased volumes or process improvements, their bottom line will take a pounding. Little wonder Alex Trotman, Ford's Chairman, acknowledged that the move had prompted 'heated discussions' with component makers.

Margin erosion has forced suppliers to cut costs, re-engineer their operations and streamline business processes. But such reorganizations were akin to 'shutting the stable door after the horse had bolted'. The suppliers had failed to identify the routes by which margins could be defended, so were left frantically chasing the business.

Buyers are spoilt for choice. They are stronger, smarter and find it easier to terminate the supplier relationship. The balance of power has shifted in the customer's favour. The change in circumstances was nicely summarized by the Sales Director of one of the world's leading computer manufacturers:

> In the early '80s we could treat the customers badly but they would always come back or we could find new ones. Today we need the customers more than they need us.

As customer choice expands and sophistication increases suppliers will face continued margin erosion while being required to provide better customer service. In this environment suppliers need to clearly understand where the profits reside within the customer base. Otherwise suppliers will attempt to be all things to all customers, will slip up and will probably go bust.

CUSTOMER BASE FRAGMENTATION

The customer base is fragmenting. Big customers are bigger and the demands placed on a supplier's front-line (marketing, sales, service and product management departments) are becoming more varied. Some customers seek a long-term partner while others are promiscuous. As the size and complexity of the customer base polarizes, the likelihood of carrying unprofitable customers increases.

Polarization by size

Across a broad spectrum of industries the customer base is polarizing. Suppliers are making a higher proportion of their sales to a smaller group of 'key accounts'. Figure 2.4 shows how the dependency on key accounts has increased for four UK manufacturers.

Increased dependency can often result from concentration within a market. For example, in the UK grocery industry the five major multiple retailers increased their share of grocery sales from 31 per cent in 1970 to 69 per cent in 1997.

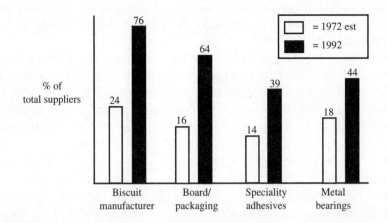

Figure 2.4   Big customers are getting bigger: sales to top five customers (including retailers) as a per cent of total supplier sales 1972–92.

Meanwhile, in the US toy industry five retailers now account for more than 50 per cent of the market. Moreover, some key accounts have grown to be substantial businesses in their own right. For example, Walmart is worth more to Procter and Gamble than some of the P&G operating countries. Similarly, the largest accounts for DHL and IBM are larger in turnover than some of their national operating units.

Another factor has been the rationalization of supplier bases. Ford cut the number of suppliers by 45 per cent between 1988 and 1992. During the same period Motorola cut suppliers by 60 per cent and BhS department store by 50 per cent. Supplier rationalization has been implemented to improve quality, lower prices or enhance supply chain efficiency. Acute suppliers have capitalized on this process to forge stronger relationships with the customer. However, this trend usually results in the customer having the upper hand, ie the risk of losing the business will hurt the supplier's bottom line more than the risk to the customer if it does not receive supply.

To illustrate the impact of customer base polarization, let us re-examine the printing supplier. The real size of its top 30 customers increased threefold between 1980 and 1992. Meanwhile, there was a boom in the number of small print shops. These start-ups expanded the overall customer base but reduced the average size of the smallest customers by approximately four-fifths.

In 1980 the largest customer was five times the size of the smallest. By 1992 this gap had grown to 60 times. The polarization in size was accompanied by a change in expectations. Large customers required key account managers and dedicated service support. Meanwhile, the small customers wanted attention. (Although £12,000 was 'small fry' to the supplier, to the customer it was a major investment.) Polarization caused the printing supplier's sales and service departments to become stretched over a wider range of customers with a more diverse and complex set of requirements. The sales organization found itself in a perpetual state of reorganization to deal with the problem.

A similar trend has occurred in the market for temporary staff. In the 1980s most contracts were held between the local factory and the local 'temp' supplier. Large employers like ICI and British Telecom were frustrated by the high costs of administration and varying standards of service between different locations. In response, Manpower Inc, the world's largest temporary staff supplier, developed national contracts, guaranteed a national standard of service and reduced the overall costs to the employer. The size of contracts increased substantially. Selling shifted from the local retail outlet to the national key account, and the consistency, professionalism and client intimacy increased.

Polarization by need

Customer needs are fragmenting. In an attempt to improve cost efficiency, quality and responsiveness, suppliers and customers have forged new ways of working together. Partnerships, new buying structures and the harnessing of modern communication systems have restructured the supplier/customer relationship. Figure 2.5 illustrates some of the changes that are taking place.

Partners or combatants?

Many customers and suppliers are looking to redefine traditional responsibilities. In most cases it is the customers that

LEVEL	OBJECTIVES	NEW RELATIONSHIP STRUCTURE
Board Room	• Improve quality, responsiveness and cost efficiency • Share risks re. R&D, stock and capital	**Partnership**
Buyers' Office	• Customize product/service to customer requirements • Work together to improve supply chain efficiency	**Co-operation/joint supply chain initiatives**
Factory Floor	• Accelerate product information/payments etc • Improve distribution efficiency	**New information transfer/ product handling systems eg EDI**

Figure 2.5 New ways of working.

Source: Abberton Associates.

are driving the change. Partnership allows them to consolidate volumes and use fewer, better suppliers. This minimizes the total costs of buying from and working with a supplier. The Japanese automotive manufacturers were pioneers of customer-driven partnership. For example, Nissan works with its suppliers to improve production processes. Nissan engineers helped one such partner, Rearsby Automotive, to cut the assembly time for a gear shift by 70 per cent. Both partners shared the cost and service benefits.

The benefits for the supplier being involved in a partnership are 'ever green contracts', increased sales, joint product development and reduced total cost of production. It also can give the supplier a unique insight into their customers' requirements. This can further build sales, improve customer retention and reduce customer sales/service costs, thereby increasing profits. These benefits need to be offset against more demanding service requirements, increased customer-specific investment, the disclosure of sensitive information and reduced supplier freedom. Despite these problems, partnership is usually more profitable for a supplier than a combative relationship.

Despite the growth of partnerships, some customers still focus on negotiating the lowest unit price, even if this sacrifices other benefits such as ease of handling, security of supply, etc. Herein lies the rub for the supplier: how can it be a partner to one customer while fighting with another to secure the best deal?

The problem becomes more complex when a supplier is selling a 'basket of goods' which have different relative values to the customer. For example, a chemicals firm can sell commodity chemicals like sulphuric acid which are very price sensitive. It can also sell 'specification chemicals' which carry proprietary brands and formulas. These command higher prices and tend to be more difficult to directly compare with competitive products. There are also 'speciality chemicals' which are tailored to the specific requirements of an individual customer. For example, a chemical engineer might work with an adhesive label manufacturer to design a glue which will provide the exact sealing and releasing properties that the manufacturer requires. This requires customer-specific investment and development. The customer can purchase commodity, specification and speciality products from the same supplier. To win the order, each product type might require a radically different level of selling and support. This complexity needs to be carefully managed to ensure that the profitability of each type of product is maximized. Such problems mean that a partnership can be difficult to forge and preserve.

New structures

The creation of the Boeing 777 illustrates how suppliers and customers have forged new relationship structures. For the first time Boeing customers were actively involved at all the stages of the new plane's design. British Airways and United Airlines engineers worked alongside Boeing's experts to ensure that the 777 would be easier to service and operate. This required Boeing to share information with suppliers and customers which previously would have been deemed 'top secret'.

Bose Corp in the US has also been restructuring the supplier/customer relationship. Frustration with the inefficiency of the traditional buyer/seller relationship prompted Bose Corp to introduce 'implants'. These staff are employed by the suppliers, but work in the Bose head office. The supplier sales department and the Bose buying office have been superseded by the 'implants', who sign Bose orders, attend product engineering meetings and work with Bose to improve the efficiency of production. The benefits for suppliers have been profound. It gives them the opportunity to work intimately with a progressive company.

Centralization of buying

Across a broad spectrum of industries decision making is being concentrated. For example, in the 1970s UK grocery manufacturers employed thousands of salespeople who called on individual outlets and the supplier would deliver the product to the shop. In the 1980s multiple grocers centralized buying at the head office and insisted that sales representatives should not call at outlets. They also demanded that deliveries should be made to a central warehouse rather than to individual shops. This allowed retailers to extract an extra 3 per cent distribution charge from the supplier.

New technology

Computers and new communication systems are having a profound impact on the buyer/seller relationship. To witness the pace of change consider the developments in the world financial markets. Contact was face-to-face and the paperwork was cumbersome and time-consuming. Today the markets rely upon the telephone, the computer and electronic payment. Millions more transactions can be handled each day, the real costs of transactions have fallen and the speed of exchange has accelerated.

The bleeper, mobile phone and computer have become indispensable in the modern financial markets. Just as the technological revolution in the financial markets bought immense change in the 1980s similar developments will be seen in the late 1990s. An easy to use share dealing system on the Internet could be cheaper, faster and more fun for an investor to use than contacting a broker. These changes in the financial markets reflect some of the new technologies which are moulding the buyer/seller relationship (Figure 2.6).

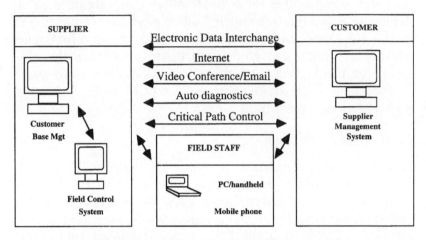

Figure 2.6   New technology at the interface.

For example, Walmart the US retail giant, has an electronic data interchange (EDI) link with all its suppliers. The paperwork associated with buying and selling has been short-circuited and information is passed quickly and accurately over the wire. This allows buyers and sellers to focus on growing sales and controlling costs. Meanwhile, in the 1980s Dell and Gateway 2000, the US computer firms, employed modern technology to radically reduce the costs of selling and serving the customer. Rather than using dealers, these companies used the telephone and Internet to forge a direct relationship with customers. Telesales and centralized helplines were used instead of agents and field personnel to link directly with customers. The benefits include:

▨   a cost of sales which is one-fifth that of a conventional PC agent-based supplier;

▨   improved intelligence – Dell has telephone contact with some 30,000 customers a day which gives it fantastic market intelligence;

▨   customer service – the telephone customer service operation can answer 90 per cent of user problems in six minutes (this compares favourably with the 20–30 per cent success rate for dealers who use the telephone but lack the Dell expert systems);

for three consecutive years, Dell has won the *PC User* magazine award for best customer service.

Dell has also pioneered the Internet as a means of selling to and serving customers. This medium can cost effectively address the needs of the small home user who seeks an upgrade. Equally, it is an effective way of serving key accounts. For example MCI saved 15 per cent by adopting the Dell Internet service whilst customer service was improved. Prior to Internet ordering, it often took MCI four-six weeks between completion of a purchase order and the delivery of a new machine. This meant that new employees could be without a computer. Through adopting the Internet order system from Dell, this time was cut to a couple of days. The success of this lower cost/higher service formula is formidable. In 1997 Dell's internet sales exceeded $1 billion, which has helped Dell become the largest supplier of desktop PCs to corporations in the US.

On a smaller scale, the use of mobile phones, pagers, e-mail, customer 'hot lines' and computerized customer management systems have allowed organizations to change the way field sales and service staff work. These tools give suppliers faster more reliable information which can be used to increase control of 'front-line' activities, accelerate cash flow, improve product management and enhance customer service. Those suppliers which have the imagination, flexibility and drive to exploit the new technology will have a real advantage versus those suppliers which are playing by the old rules of the game.

Unfortunately, customers will move at different speeds which means that suppliers could be left bearing the costs of old and new technology. The supplier can either develop new service structures to accommodate these varying needs or it can focus on certain types of customer. Either way, the complexity increases as does the capacity to 'get it wrong'. In these circumstances a creative and careful management of the customer base and front-line divisions becomes critical.

INCREASING COSTS OF THE INTERFACE

Most companies do not monitor the full costs of interfacing with the customer. Instead they compartmentalize the costs into marketing, sales, service and administration budgets. However, one customer might require more work from the accounts department than another or the R&D investment in a specific customer might be very high. A company needs to look at the total costs associated with serving the customer. When all these costs are loaded in the supplier can often find that it is spending more than 20–30 per cent of its turnover on 'interface' costs (Figure 2.7).

The costs are further increased if the manufacturer builds in any reseller or retail margins that the final customer is paying. For example, let's take a product as simple as a newspaper. Of the 80 pence spent by the customer on *The Financial Times* 26.5 per cent will be taken by the retailer. A further 10 per cent

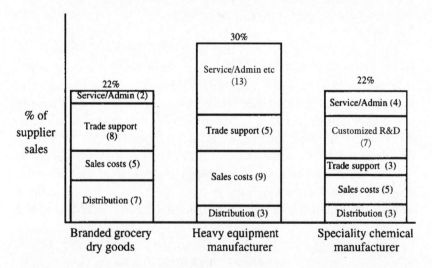

Figure 2.7　Costs of serving the customer as a per cent of total manufacturing sales 1994 (direct service to retailer/customer – excludes the use of intermediaries, wholesalers, etc).

Source: Suppliers in each sector with average sales £70 million.

will be taken by the wholesaler for delivering the copies to the retailer. To this must be added the costs of distribution to the wholesaler, selling costs, admin costs and trade promotions. In total, more than 50 per cent of the customer's spend has been absorbed by the 'interface'.

Given the total level of cost invested at the interface, surprisingly little senior management time is focused on improving this area of the business. Partly for this reason it appears that 'interface' costs have been allowed to inflate ahead of other manufacturer costs. Several factors are contributing to this. The costs of front line staff are increasing, productivity gains have been slower than in other parts of the supplier organization and the indirect costs associated with serving customers are escalating.

Cost of front-line staff is increasing

Marketing, sales, service and distribution departments are labour intensive. The costs of these people tend to be rising at a faster rate than selling prices. This has been illustrated by the *Sales and Marketing Management* survey of the costs of a sales representative. This survey examines thousands of companies in the US and has found that the real costs of a sales executive have increased by 12 per cent in the early 1990s. In Europe the real costs have risen at a faster rate than in the US due to real wage inflation and higher tax rates.

Lack of technology

Interface departments have been relatively slow to harness computer technology. While most production plants and accounting offices are driven by the computer, only a minority of firms have gained benefit from utilizing IT in marketing, sales and service operations. Although organizations are adopting new technology to increase productivity. The explosion of pagers, mobile phones, lap top computers and call centres bears testimony to this trend. However, despite this huge investment in technology, the total costs of selling tend to be increasing and many organizations have difficulty quantifying the real, bottom line payback from this investment.

Customer solutions

Customers increasingly want solutions rather than products. Customization ranges from delivering in customer-determined pack sizes to tailoring a service/product to meet the specific needs of a user. Take, for example, buying a car from Rover. In the 1970s a customer would visit the show room during 'regular working hours'. Today a test car can be dropped off at the customer's home or office. Rather than buying the car that is displayed, it can be customized to reflect the customer's needs (ie colour of interior, shape of seat, etc). Thus the dealer is offering 'special' rather than 'standard' services while the manufacturer is 'customizing' the product rather than selling 'off the shelf'.

This change is fundamental to the way the business operates. Rather than the manufacturing line being set up to produce thousands of identical units, on a given day it can produce cars which are adjusted to meet customer needs. The dealer's role has changed from selling a mass produced item to diagnosing the customer's needs and wants and tailoring a profitable solution.

Customization places increased pressure on 'front-line departments'. They need to diagnose the customer requirements and then work with product management, R&D and finance to construct a profitable solution. An increasing proportion of a product's cost structure is therefore being invested in specific customers. This increases the risk costs associated with the management of an individual customer. This risk is accentuated if the supplier makes any of the following mistakes:

▓ *Over-promising.* In their eagerness to 'close a sale' sales staff can over-commit to a customer.

▓ *Misunderstandings.* When adaptation to a product/service is being undertaken on behalf of a customer it is essential that the customization is fully agreed between the two parties.

▓ *Wrong answers.* In 1994 the London Ambulance Service

suffered the disaster that its new computerized call management system failed to work properly. After at least one fatality, it dumped the new system and commenced legal proceedings against the software supplier. The system was nearly good enough, but this was useless in a life and death business. The software industry, like construction and other customer solution businesses, is littered with suppliers who have diagnosed the wrong answer and have paid the penalty.

Wrong customer. When Laker Airlines went bust, one unfortunate crockery supplier was left with over a million pounds worth of ceramics 'which were of no use to anybody . . . they had Laker written all over them and they were made for airline portions'.

As suppliers produce solutions, they must either face the liabilities of 'getting it wrong', or they must invest in the organization, systems and people to 'get it right'. This is not as easy as it sounds. If a business has been set up to 'push' a product to a wide variety of customers it is difficult to develop the skills to respond to individual customer requirements. This change in mentality, organization, structure and operations can prove expensive and increase overall interface costs.

Litigation and corruption

Unhappy customers have become more expensive. UK pension companies have been forced to pay compensation for salespeople giving bad advice to prospective customers. In the United States the courts are bogged down with customers suing suppliers for misadvice, late delivery, poor performance, etc. There is also the problem of corruption at the front line. Sales managers have always kept a keen eye on the fiddling of expenses yet in the 1990s we have seen corruption hit the big time. At Barings bank, Nick Leeson traded the company into a £600 million liability. Less attention has been drawn to the cases of salespeople taking 'back handers' for losing a sale or awarding unduly large discounts to a customer in response to a special incentive. These liabilities erode profits and increase insurance and legal fees.

Inflation of direct and indirect interface costs can be substantial. As Figure 2.8 shows, many firms have seen interface costs increase as a proportion of turnover. As these costs inflate, so the risk that a competitor might use technology to offer a lower cost/higher service solution increases.

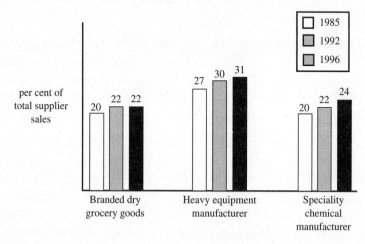

Figure 2.8   Costs of serving the customer as per cent of total manufacturer sales 1985 vs 1992.

Source: Four companies/divisions in each sector; combined turnover of sample = £1.6 billion.

TRADE CHANNELS AT WAR

A supplier can employ a variety of routes to reach the customer. It might sell direct or use agents, wholesalers and retailers. Each channel might have radically different economics and provide a unique customer service. For example, a customer can buy a can of Coca Cola from a vending machine, a retailer or in a restaurant.

Trade channel management is becoming more complex. Computer technology and the telephone allow suppliers to sell direct to their customers thereby 'cutting out' resellers and retailers. Meanwhile, retailers are developing private label brands thereby 'de-listing' some branded suppliers.

As the customer base fragments and new channel structures are formed, a supplier can find that its trade channels start to fight between themselves for profit. The net loser tends to be the supplier and potentially the final customer. The supplier must carefully manage its trade channels to maximize profits and enhance the service to the final customer.

Going direct

The adoption of the telephone, Internet and direct mail has allowed suppliers to go direct to customers rather than using agents, resellers and retailers.

British Airways, Apple Computers, Guardian Insurance and Levis have all introduced direct selling systems which compete with traditional, indirect channels. This requires the supplier to develop the new 'skill set' of working directly with customers whilst having to appease and motivate the conventional indirect selling systems. Meanwhile, Barclays bank offers the customer a variety of banking options. The customer can use a conventional branch service or can bank via the telephone, the PC or the Internet. Each route is charged in a different way. Barclays seeks to ensure that the customer is not confused by this array of options whilst ensuring that each channel optimizes profits.

Trade channel management

Successful trade management has become essential in determining corporate success. For example, for much of the 1970s and 1980s Golden Wonder was the UK's largest supplier of potato crisps. In an attempt to maximize sales, it developed a complex variety of channels to get to the market. Independent retailers could buy from Golden Wonder's van selling operation, via a cash and carry, via a delivered wholesaler or via a buying group. Each of the channels was eager to win the business and fought to improve service or lower the cost price.

This left the retailer bamboozled. One month it was best to buy off the van and the next from a wholesaler. The channels were so busy fighting amongst themselves that they failed to notice that Walkers Crisps had 'stolen a march'. It focused its limited selling resources on developing retailers and the cash and carry sector. The Walkers sales representatives would call on retailers and encourage them to purchase Walkers from the cash and carry. All the selling power was focused on driving out the competition rather than fighting with other trade channels. It placed all its sales via the cash and carry sector which was the fastest growing trade channel. Although at the time it was a smaller brand than Golden Wonder, in the cash and carry trade it quickly grew to be number one. It therefore received more trade support which accelerated Walkers expansion.

Moreover, because Walkers only employed one channel it could minimize its interface costs. This gave Walkers a major cost advantage versus Golden Wonder and allowed Walkers to keep a tighter control on trade activities. Tight control of the cash and carry sector ensured that inventory management was optimized. As such, Walkers ensured that its crisps were fresher than Golden Wonder which had more stock in its complex supply chain. Moreover, Walkers refused to provide discounts beyond the list price. Consequently, Walkers preserved better trade margins than other crisp suppliers. These cost savings and favourable margins were reinvested in brand support and into preserving a superior product. Consequently, Walkers developed a much stronger brand franchise than competitive products. This combination of factors allowed Walkers to secure market leadership with an advantaged business system.

Private label

Trade channel management has even become more complex since retailers and resellers embarked on the development of 'private label'. In an attempt to improve margins, increase price competitiveness and leverage their own brand investment, resellers and retailers have increased the mix of exclusive/private label products. For example, in the UK grocery business over 55 per cent of sales are own label. In sectors such as cotton wool and ambient ready meals, over 85 per cent of sales are own label. As such they have become the major threat to branded suppliers.

The private label threat is seen across a broad spectrum of industries including clothing, groceries, food, office supplies, over-the-counter drugs, auto replacement parts and computer peripherals. In each case the reseller is deskilling the supplier. Design, branding, R&D and other value-added activities are passing down the chain to the reseller leaving the supplier as a contracted manufacturer.

The irony of the private label threat is that it was partly the result of branded supplier, trade channel management. Had not branded suppliers awarded Sainsbury's and Safeway's superior margins in the 1960s, 1970s and 1980s it is unlikely that they would have expanded so quickly. The superior margins were invested in new stores and systems which allowed the retail chains to expand quickly. This growth allowed retailers to demand superior margins from branded suppliers while launching private label products. Of course, private label manufacturing can be a highly profitable business. For example, the clothing and food producers which manufacture for Marks & Spencer make a higher return on capital than most branded suppliers within their market sectors. However, the private label business requires a different costing system and corporate philosophy to that of selling branded products. As such, it requires very careful strategic and trade channel management.

Channel price fighting

Another issue arises if the channels use a product as a 'loss leader' to generate sales of other higher margin products. This was witnessed in 1996 in parts of the UK software market. Suppliers found that mail order and telephone selling companies were selling software at a 20 per cent discount to the manufacturer's recommended retail price. High street retailers worried about appearing expensive and price matched against the direct channels. As a result the profitability of the retailers declined and they demanded additional promotional support from the supplier. The supplier was left with three options: either face delisting by the retail trade channels which would threaten sales, suffer reduced margins or differentiate the retailed product from that which is sold via mail order. Whichever route was adopted the suppliers' profits were eroded.

Front-line staff turning 'native'

If a key account manager is bonused on the sales growth that is achieved through his or her account they will eagerly seek promotion support to cultivate sales via that channel. They will also call on other departments to focus resources on boosting the sales of the individual account. This can result in key account managers competing against each other which forces the supplier to increase account-specific investment. If this competition shifts sales from one channel to another rather than growing overall demand, there is a real danger that the supplier ends up giving more money/effort to the individual accounts which erodes long-term profitability.

New competition

The supplier needs to be constantly on guard against new competitors which 'cherry pick' the most profitable customers within a market. Through employing clever customer targeting strategies and low cost/high service customer management systems they can target the most profitable customers within a market.

One such example was Dell computers. In the early 1980s Michael Dell recognized that there was a large group of sophisticated computer buyers who were forced to buy computers via expensive dealers despite them not requiring dealer services. These customers spent more than an average customer yet required less service support. Dell used the telephone and a direct distribution system to provide the service these customers required at a cost which was 20 per cent below a conventional dealer. It successfully grew to be a $5 billion business leaving the dealers with the expensive-to-serve customers. The Dell system was so successful that most of the major manufacturers had to reduce agent margins and set up their own direct selling systems.

Cherry picking is also common in the financial services sector. Charles Schwab in the US recognized that there was a large group of private investors who were paying brokerage fees for services they did not use. He targeted these customers with a limited option, over-the-phone, discount brokerage service. It has now grown to be a multi-billion business and has taken from the banks and brokers some of their most profit-able customers. The system has been continually refined. For example, Charles Schwab was one of the pioneers of the Internet as a means of reaching sophisticated customers via a lower cost service. Today Charles Schwab has more than one million internet customers with over $80 billion of funds under management. In fact, nearly half of the trades executed by Charles Schwab, in the first quarter of 1998, were conducted on line. This compared with approximately one third in the first quarter of 1997. This direct infrastructure is now being harnessed to sell new services. For example, Charles Schwab is exploring the opportunity to sell other banking and financial services. Similarly, in 1989 First Direct bank (a subsidiary of Midland Plc) was established. It targeted customers with high disposable incomes and reasonable risk profiles who did not need to go into a bank branch. Through the incentive of lower bank charges and an excellent telephone-based service it has won over 0.6 million of the UK's most profitable banking customers.

Across a broad spectrum of industries, slick 'cherry pickers' are using new technology to target the most profitable customers within a market and then provide them with a superior service. This leaves traditional suppliers scrambling to 'lock in' core customers or serving the unprofitable rump of the customer base.

SUMMARY

In a detailed examination of six major UK corporations it transpired that after allocating the appropriate sales margins and servicing costs, between 14 and 32 per cent of customers were unprofitable (see Figure 2.8). Some customers, when treated on a marginal basis, made a positive contribution to overheads, and some unprofitable customers were 'development accounts' which would make a positive return in the future. These cus-

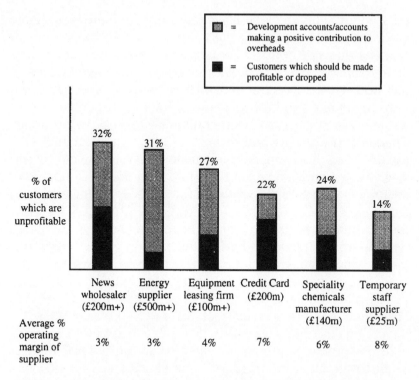

Figure 2.9 Percentage of unprofitable customers after the allocation of customer service costs.
Source: Abberton Associates survey of six UK companies.

tomers could be 'carried' whereas between 4 and 15 per cent needed to be turned around to be profitable or dropped.

Conversely, the companies were drawing between 30 and 140 per cent of their profits from the top 10 per cent of accounts. In each case the company was very exposed to a small group of core customers. Moreover, each of the companies had seen a higher proportion of their profits coming from a smaller group of customers than a decade ago. The gap between profitable and unprofitable customers had widened. Of course, a sample of six companies is too small on which to base firm conclusions. Yet in a survey of over 200 major UK firms, 74 per cent of sales directors claimed that serving the needs of key accounts was at the top of their sales agenda for the next five years. It appears that the majority of sales directors have recognized that the profit within their customer base is becoming more concentrated.

Management of the customer base is increasingly difficult. The customer base is less predictable as customers can switch supplier at little risk. Customers are smarter and demand better service requiring suppliers to absorb more customer-specific costs and risks. Meanwhile, the customer base is polarizing with the supplier being more dependent on a core group of profitable customers. These factors mean that the front line has got to be capable of serving a more complex and disparate set of customer needs. Add to this the risk that the trade channels are fighting against each other just when a cherry picker attempts to grab the core profit customers and you enter the nightmare scenario. But it is not all bad news. In earlier times it would have been virtually impossible for large corporations to manage small groups of customers or tailor the offer to individual customer's needs. Instead they were set up to manage 'products and markets'. The computer revolution has given suppliers the capacity to manage the profit opportunities within the customer base. This has opened the doors to new sources of profit. In this new, exciting environment, effective management of the customer base becomes essential in determining corporate success.

3

IS THERE A PROBLEM?

There are five simple diagnostics which allow an organization to review whether it has a problem or is missing opportunities with its customer base:

1. *Interview a few customers.* Some managers might use consultants, market research firms or sales staff to find out what customers are saying. These routes are too far removed. It is better for a senior manager to formally interview some key customers. The interviews should formally rate the organization in all the key service criteria, ie responsiveness, quality, price, etc, with the objective of seeing whether customers are 'delighted', 'happy', 'satisfied' or about to give up. Usually six customer meetings with people from different levels within the customer organization will give a good enough 'snapshot' of the existing customer base. It is also worth interviewing four or so potential customers which presently buy from a competitor. This will help review the relative competitive threat. Finally, be brave enough to interview five or so customers which have ceased trading with your organization in the past couple of years. Their views will prove invaluable.

2. *Call up your sales office pretending to be a new account.* Three minutes of listening to an answerphone playing Mozart or a conversation with a disinterested secretary will confirm that the company is in trouble. A similar exercise with the competition will clarify whether they are servicing their new accounts more or less effectively.

3. *Ask the marketing, sales or finance director to tell you the value of the top ten and bottom ten accounts/customer groups.* If this cannot be provided within an hour it is reasonable to assume that the organization is failing to manage the customer base. Then ask them if your competition has customers which are more or less profitable than your own? What is the reason for the difference? If they do not know, your firm is probably missing some significant opportunities.

4. *Ask the marketing and sales directors: 'How long does it usually take for us to make a profit on a new customer?'* If the answer is 'immediately' or 'it's difficult to tell' your firm is failing to manage the customer lifecycle.

5. *Ask the heads of R&D and product management: 'What share of the customer's pocket do we currently have and what is the target for five years' time?' and 'What was the customer involvement in our last major product development initiative?'* If the response is reserved, the customer base is not being used to channel customer intelligence and your staff are not thinking about the profit opportunities that reside within the customer base.

These 'diagnostics' can be completed in a few days. They should give an idea as to whether the organization could refine its management of the customer base. Having identified whether there is an opportunity the supplier can explore seven steps to increasing the profitability of the customer base (see Figure 3.1).

The first step is to identify who your customers are and to evaluate their current and future value. The organization should then seek to lock in and develop the core profit accounts. After all, the loss of a core profit account can do more damage than successfully recruiting 10 new customers. With the core profit customers secure, the supplier can focus on increasing income. Can it increase its share of the customer's pocket? What can be done to increase the frequency of purchase and average transaction values? What value can be added to increase profitable income? What new customers should be targeted? Should the pricing structures be refined?

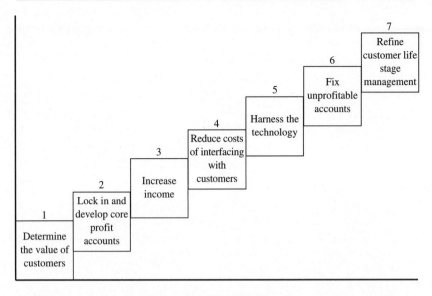

Figure 3.1   Steps to increasing profits via customer base management.

Having obtained a clear understanding of where the current and potential profit resides within the customer base, management can focus on optimizing the costs of interfacing with customer. The supplier must be confident that it is not wasting effort or carrying surplus cost within its front-line divisions. It cannot afford to be covering the wrong customers at the wrong time or be doing the wrong things. Otherwise it is exposed to cherry pickers finding a more cost-effective route to delight the profitable customers. The supplier can then deal with any unprofitable customers. The final step is to refine customer life stage management, ie effectively develop the customer from its initial recruitment to the time the relationship ceases.

This continual rethinking and tighter focusing of customer base management is not easy. However, this systematic approach should help unlock any hidden profits.

4

DETERMINING THE VALUE
OF A CUSTOMER

Prior to improving customer base management the organization must understand where the current and future profits reside. Precisely understanding the future value of a customer is impossible. In 1970 no dry goods supplier would have predicted that a small chain in Arkansas would grow to be the world's biggest retailer. Likewise a shop assistant in London in 1995 could not have predicted that an Arab prince would buy all of a store's stock in one afternoon. Despite the inherent unpredictability of customer behaviour, the supplier should strive to evaluate the relative attractiveness of different customers/groups of customers.

A tool which can help address this question is 'discounted customer profitability'. This attempts to quantify the total current and expected value of the customer base. Figure 4.1 shows how DCP is calculated. DCP is not a scientific analysis and requires a lot of estimates and judgements. However, by formally considering the components of customer profitability the supplier develops a more intricate understanding of where the profit opportunities reside.

COMPONENTS OF CUSTOMER PROFITABILITY

The customer

As soon as you start to review customer profitability a fundamental question will arise. Who is the customer? Is it the end

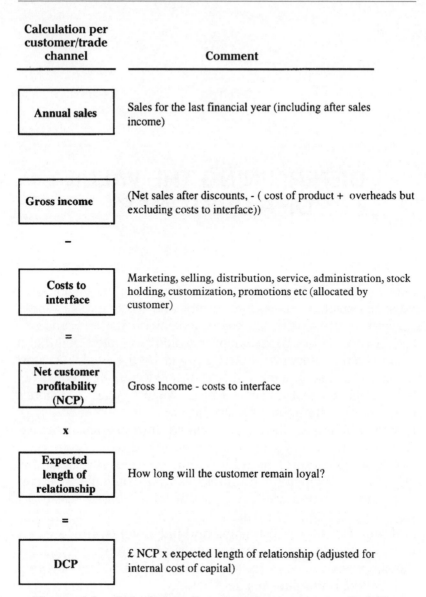

Calculation per customer/trade channel	Comment
Annual sales	Sales for the last financial year (including after sales income)
Gross income	(Net sales after discounts, - (cost of product + overheads but excluding costs to interface))
–	
Costs to interface	Marketing, selling, distribution, service, administration, stock holding, customization, promotions etc (allocated by customer)
=	
Net customer profitability (NCP)	Gross Income - costs to interface
x	
Expected length of relationship	How long will the customer remain loyal?
=	
DCP	£ NCP x expected length of relationship (adjusted for internal cost of capital)

Figure 4.1   Calculating discounted customer profitability.

user, or the person who signs the cheque made out to the supplier? Brand managers talk of the householder as being the customer, whereas sales staff often call the retailer the customer. To keep things simple for the present, let's consider the customer as being the person who pays the supplier's invoice.

However, a separate analysis of final customer profitability and trade channel profitability might be required.

In some cases the supplier will have such a huge customer base that it is impractical to review the behaviour of each individual customer. The supplier should instead obtain a profile of typical customer groups. Suppliers need to be careful when identifying a customer group. A marketeer might immediately consider socio-demographic segments as being the customer groups. Equally it might be appropriate to segment according to the service used, the amount spent or the service requirements of a customer. As an example think about the customers in a pub. A market segment could be women aged 25–35 who drink alcohol and are price sensitive. However, these need to be segmented according to whether they are lunchtime versus evening customers, or those that are in a rush versus those which stay all night and those which are regulars versus infrequents. This segmentation will require detailed consideration. In some cases the customer clusters become so complex that it is easier to manage the individual customer.

Annual sales

In theory it should be relatively simple to calculate the sales that a supplier makes to its customer. Yet if the supplier and customer have multiple divisions across different countries, matters can become complex. For example, when undertaking this analysis for a global chemicals firm, ICI's name appeared in the sales ledger of numerous divisions. When all these sales were totalled up ICI accounted for more than 10 per cent of total sales. The supplier should also incorporate the value of any service contracts or other indirect sources of income from the customer.

Some organizations which have particularly large customer bases might argue that they cannot identify individual customer sales. A retailer or a chain of fast-food outlets might have millions of customers, each of which makes a series of individual transactions. It is difficult to determine how much an individual spends over the course of a year. However, if the customer spends more than £100 per annum it could be worth setting up a customer database. For example, Tesco (the UK grocer) has amassed the details of six million customers while Blockbuster video has more than 35 million customers on its database. Tesco can identify where a customer lives, when and where they shop and even whether they prefer Coke or Pepsi. As the cost effectiveness of database management improves, most organizations will be able to monitor the performance of individual customers.

Gross income

The gross income of a particular account should also be easy to calculate. However, the supplier needs to be sure that it fully allocates any overriders, retrospectives or promotional discounts. When this analysis was undertaken at a potato snack manufacturer it emerged that some accounts were receiving additional discounts which totalled more than 10 per cent of sales. The result was that some small accounts were receiving a lower net buying price than major grocery customers. Many of these customers turned out to be unprofitable.

Costs to interface

The supplier needs to carefully allocate all the costs associated with interfacing with and serving a customer. This requires the identification of all 'direct charges' such as selling and service time, free samples, etc. But it also requires indirect charges like customer-specific R&D, marketing, late payment costs, etc. For example, a breakdown of the costs-to-interface with a customer for a supplier to the European print industry is shown in Figure 4.2.

Interestingly, there was a significant deviation between two apparently similar customers. A sixth of the customer base had costs-to-serve which totalled more than 41 per cent of sales. Meanwhile, another sixth of customers had a cost-to-serve that was less than 17 per cent of sales. This deviation in the needs and costs of similar customers was essential in determining future resource requirements.

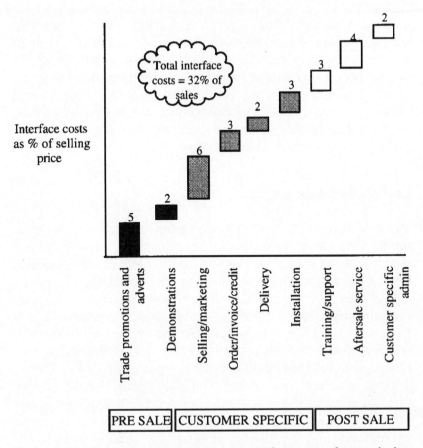

Interface costs as % of selling price

Total interface costs = 32% of sales

Trade promotions and adverts — 5
Demonstrations — 2
Selling/marketing — 6
Order/invoice/credit — 3
Delivery — 2
Installation — 3
Training/support — 3
Aftersale service — 4
Customer specific admin — 2

| PRE SALE | CUSTOMER SPECIFIC | POST SALE |

Figure 4.2   Interface costs as per cent of turnover for a printing equipment supplier.

Calculating total costs-to-serve is often resisted by front-line managers. It is seen as time-consuming and they claim that a large proportion of time is 'unallocated'. Beware of unallocated time: if front-line effort cannot be tied back to a specific customer it usually highlights a sloppy deployment of resources.

Net customer profitability

Having obtained the true income and costs of serving different customers, the supplier can review the level of profits being generated by the different parts of the base. Customers with similar profiles of income and costs-to-serve can be grouped into 'customer clusters' or into trade channels. It is useful to create a customer league table to see which customers/groups appear at the top and the bottom. This might provoke some obvious opportunities. Why does one customer have a significantly higher interface cost than another? Why is one customer getting a better margin than another?

Length of relationship

The length of the expected relationship is important in determining the value of the customer. The value of a customer over its lifetime can be huge: a frequent flyer often spends more than £20,000 with British Airways over a 10-year period, a loyal Visa member can spend more than £50,000 on the card over the duration of the relationship, and a regular at a pub can have a lifetime value in excess of £7000. In business to business selling the customers can be colossal. British Airways has spent billions with Boeing and the US Defense Department has spent tens of billions with IBM. It is only through viewing the relationship over time that the full value of the customer is appreciated.

Predicting the length and value of the relationships is not easy. Will the customer produce a steady stream of income for the next 20 years or will it go bust in a few months' time? You can 'guestimate' the length of relationship as follows:

▊ Calculate the average length of customer relationship, ie 1, 3, 5, 10 or 15 years.

▊ Undertake a customer survey to identify the probability of customers buying again from your firm in the future. This will identify those customers which have an above or below average life expectancy.

▊ Ask the sales people to conduct a simple business review of their customers, ie how they are placed within the market, new requirements, etc.

With the above information the management team can estimate the robustness of the customer relationship relative to
the 'average customer'. This analysis will 'flag up' high-risk
accounts.

Calculating the customer's expected lifespan is further complicated if your customer has customers. A factor in determining the longevity and size of your business will be how your
customer is serving its own customer base. It is common
sense for your sales and marketing people to spend time evaluating the destiny of your customers' customers. Incorporate
this process into the DCP review to understand how robust
each customer's business appears to be.

The task is made more complex if the customer has a
'peaky' sales pattern. As an example consider the difference
between the buyer of a car and the loyal customer at a grocery
store. The grocery store will have weekly contact with the customer. It is quite easy to see whether the customer is reducing
his or her spend and the store can respond accordingly. The
auto dealer has the problem that the customer could make a
purchase of £15,000 this week and might not be seen again.

Although the auto customer has a more peaky demand profile, the dealer should attempt to cement a solid, ongoing relationship after the car has been sold. This will bear fruit when the
customer decides to repurchase. This probability of repurchasing should be factored into the lifetime value of the customer.

Discounted Customer Profitability

Having estimated the length of the relationship and calculated
the net profitability, you can multiply the two to review the
total profit that the customer is expected to produce. The
future profitability should be discounted by your company's
internal cost of capital (ie profit in three years' time is not
worth as much as profit today). Moreover, if a customer's
profit is expected to change significantly over the course of the
relationship you would need to revise the margin and cost to
serve numbers accordingly. For example, the customer might
be a development account or could be in rapid decline. In

either case you need to adjust the average profitability over the life of the relationship.

Having undertaken this analysis, it is useful to put your customers in a DCP league. One fact is likely to leap out – customers are not created equal. The gap between the most profitable and least valuable customer/trade channel can often vary by a factor of ten or even hundreds. For example, a store's ranking of customers using its store credit card showed that some customers were losing the retailer £22 per annum while others were producing more than £1000 of profit. Likewise, a speciality chemicals firm discovered that the top 10 per cent of customers were worth 200 times more than the bottom 10 per cent of customers.

Estimating the current and expected profitability of a customer is essential in determining the resources that are deployed against it. However, other factors might also need to be taken into consideration. The supplier might obtain indirect benefits from the customer relationship. For example:

- ▇ **Insight.** Component suppliers to NASA have benefited from having access to research findings.

- ▇ **Expertise.** British suppliers have learnt new production process skills from Nissan which have allowed them to win contracts from other automotive firms.

- ▇ **Endorsement.** Flagship customers can help suppliers win additional business. In its early days, for example, in the 1979 election Saatchi and Saatchi obtained a high profile due to their work with the British Conservative Party.

- ▇ **Fun.** Some customers are more fun than others. A regular at a bar can help improve the atmosphere, just as a lawyer can enjoy working for one client more than another. Such customers can be motivational for staff or for other customers.

Suppliers should formally review the indirect benefits of such relationships, not merely to quantify the value of the associated PR, intelligence, etc but to review whether they can exploit further indirect benefits from the relationship. Can they learn more or sell more as a result of a particular client relationship?

USE OF DCP

The indirect benefits discussed above show that DCP is not an all-encompassing means of valuing a customer. However, DCP does help a supplier consider the relative importance and potential of different customers. As an example, we will examine the discounted customer profitability for three customers of a news wholesaler. The wholesaler receives copies of newspapers and magazines from a publisher and distributes them to the retailers. The wholesaler typically has five hundred such retail customers. In this example we have selected three types of retailer which have the same level of sales (see Figure 4.3). Although the turnover is the same, the margins and interface costs show significant deviation.

Background

Newsagent A operated effective retail systems and was based three miles from the wholesaler's premises. It required little management time and was cheap to serve. Newsagent B sold the same amount of newspaper/magazines as A; however, it employed sloppy management systems and was based 25 miles from the wholesaler. The supermarket also sold £55,000 of news products; however, it was part of a large multiple group which had negotiated favourable margins with the wholesaler. The supermarket therefore produced £1100 less margin for the wholesaler.

Costs to interface

The costs of interfacing with the outlets were determined by the amount of selling, service and administration time the accounts require. Because newsagent B was poorly managed, the wholesaler spent 25 per cent more time managing it than a typical outlet. This involved sorting out payments, estimating

	Newsagent A	Newsagent B	Supermarket (new account)
Sales (£'000s pa)	55.0	55.0	55.0
Margin %	**7.5**	**7.5**	**5.5**
Gross margin (£'000)	4.1	4.1	3.0
Costs to Interface (£'000)			
Selling	0.5	0.6	0.5
Distribution	1.5	2.2	2.0
Service	0.7	0.9	0.7
Administration	0.3	0.5	0.4
Total	**3.0**	**4.0**	**3.6**
Net customer profitability (£'000)	**1.1**	**0.1**	**(–0.6)**
Adjusted NCP (£'000)	na	na	**0.3** (increased sales)
Expected length of relationship (yrs)	5.0	3.0 (High competition will force closure)	5.0
Discounted customer profitability (£'000)[*]	5.5	0.3	1.5

[*] For ease of understanding the DCP has not been discounted by a cost of capital

Figure 4.3   Example of DCP: news wholesaler supplying news retailers.

sales, etc. As a result, the 'Net Profitability' ranged from –£600 to +£1000.

Length of relationship

The wholesaler had a five-year contract to supply newspapers to the outlets. However, Newsagent B was unlikely to survive five years due to its poor management. Due to the low margin received, the supermarket was unprofitable to serve. However, the supermarket was a development account and was anticipated to grow significantly the following year. On the basis of the revised costs it was expected to make the wholesaler £300 of profit per annum.

Discounted customer profitability

The net result of the analysis was that the discounted value of Newsagent A was £5500, versus £300 for Newsagent B and £1500 for the supermarket, ie Newsagent A was going to make three times more profit than Newsagent B and the supermarket combined! Prior to undertaking the review all three customers had been treated equally. Following the review the wholesaler invited all his Newsagent A type outlets to dinner and made sure that any problems they had were dealt with immediately. Newsagent B was trained to minimize the disruption to the wholesaler, and the supermarket was given aggressive sales targets to achieve profitability.

This is a comparatively simple example and, depending upon the industry refinements, might be required:

- in the chemicals industry, where a customer can purchase via different divisions, in different countries;

- in a computer leasing firm, which must consider the profitability of service and financing contracts;

- by a truck manufacturer, who can have a customer which buys one hundred vehicles this year and only five next year;

- by an advertising agency, which can find that a 'flag ship' account helps draw other business;

- by a credit card company, who might need to understand the bad debt risk

- an airline may need to accrue for any frequent flyer miles.

Each of these refinements will increase the precision of the DCP model to ensure that it reflects the true value of the customer.

As this example shows, a supplier can deceive itself if it monitors customers only according to their turnover. It also gives a glimpse of how an understanding of the DCP can highlight the easiest ways to defend and increase profits. Once again, it should be stressed that DCP is not a scientific process. It is a tool to help find the opportunities that reside in the customer base. A management team will often need to rely on best estimates and judgement calls when assembling the data. There are several guidelines which maximize the value of measuring customer profitability:

Sample

Before embarking on a major review of customer profitability, model the profile for a small sample. The sample should be randomly selected and probably include circa 16 customers. The income stream and costs to interface must be calculated to determine net customer profitability. The customers should then be then surveyed to established current satisfaction and the intention to purchase in the future. This information is critical in evaluating likely customer retention and it's future value. This sample serves three purposes; it identifies whether a larger analysis will be revealing, it highlights the key determinants of profitability and it allows the organization to 'ball park' the total profit benefits accruing from enhanced customer management.

Simple

Identify the key determinants of customer profitability and refine the measurement of these. In most cases, an organization does not need to measure every detail of every interface cost. By identifying the 'key drivers' the data is easier to compile and the understanding of the analysis improves. Possibly, the management might conclude that the key determinant of profitability turnover (ie the margins, costs to serve and account longevity) are strongly correlated to sales. If this is the case, the analysis can be simplified.

Co-ordinated

Responsibility for customer profitability cuts across department divisions. For example, high costs in customer installation are often the results of poor selling. As such, the analysis of customer profitability should involve representatives from sales, service, marketing, production and finance. Moreover, the results of the analysis should be jointly presented to the directors responsible for these areas. After all, improvements to customer profitability will usually require better collaboration between interface divisions and might require a re-allocation of resources from one part of the interface to another.

Profit Focused

Measuring and managing customer profitability is of no value unless it makes a major contribution to the bottom line. The analysis must explore the scope to build value through:

- locking-in core profit accounts;

- finding easy routes to building income;

- reducing the costs of interfacing with customers;

- improving the management of the customer lifestages.

The DCP model can then be re-calculated to show the profit impact of employing each of these levers in order to prioritize activity.

5

LOCK IN CORE PROFIT CUSTOMERS

The top 15 per cent of customers can often account for between 30 and 100 per cent of a supplier's profits. If such customers are lost they can have a devastating impact on the bottom line. Take, for example, the DCP of a capital goods manufacturer and a mixed goods retailer (see Figure 5.1).

In both cases the top 15 per cent of customers produce four times more DCP than an average customer. If the supplier loses a core profit customer, it will need to develop at least

Customer Type	Capital goods manufacturer DCP (£)	Mixed goods retailer DCP (£)
Average DCP of top 15% of customers (core profit accounts)	502,000	1,400
Average DCP	124,000	330
Average DCP of bottom 15% of customers	–33,000	–22
Expected DCP of a new recruit	46,000	154

Figure 5.1 Relative value of the customer base:
DCP of different types of customer.

Source: Abberton Associates research.

four average customers to make up the difference. However, new recruits are unlikely to be 'average'. Instead they will typically be development accounts which will generate a DCP somewhere between average and the bottom 15 per cent of the customer base. On this basis 10 new customers would be required to make up for the loss of a single core profit account. Given the value of a core profit customer relative to a new customer, the supplier should 'lock in' what it's got before it goes searching for new opportunities.

Suppliers can under-manage core customers due to a variety of factors. Probably the most common reason is that they confuse customer inertia with loyalty. The supplier believes that its customers are happy because they are not complaining. However, when a better competitive offer arrives these inert customers jump ship at a rapid rate. This sensitivity means that the supplier cannot afford to take loyal customers for granted. There are seven routes to 'lock in' core customers:

1. achieve and surpass current expectations;
2. elevate the relationship;
3. bond the customer to the supplier organization;
4. prepare for future needs;
5. manage customers which are in decline;
6. reward loyalty;
7. never believe that a core customer is 'safe'.

DELIVER AND SURPASS CURRENT EXPECTATIONS

There is no excuse for failing to understand and satisfy the requirements of core profit accounts. Whether through customer research, feedback from the front-line divisions or regular account reviews, the supplier must continually refine its understanding of core customers.

Listen to the customer

Sales people often pretend to listen to the customer when really they are waiting to launch into a pitch. Service departments can bombard customers with pre-printed 'satisfaction surveys' and brand managers can research a customer to death without 'bottoming' the real issues. All these front-line staff should be working together to identify the factors which are most important to the core customer and understanding how the supplier scores relative to the competition.

Obtaining meaningful, actionable feedback is difficult. Problems can arise because the supplier asks questions that it considers to be important rather than those questions which are important to the customer. Research is further complicated if there are multiple decision makers within an account. Each individual might have varying opinions regarding the importance/score. To overcome these obstacles managers should probe customers in formal interviews and focus groups prior to commissioning research.

A simple framework for pulling this intelligence together is show in Figure 5.2. It summarizes research that was undertaken on behalf of a major, temporary staff supplier. It shows how 'importance' can be plotted against the 'rating' to identify the key areas for improvement.

The customers were mainly large UK public limited companies. Overall, the supplier was doing an excellent job but there was scope for improvement. For example, 'proactive management' was deemed important by clients yet the supplier's score was below average. Customers wanted the early identification of problems and effective management of the issue rather than waiting until it became a last minute crisis. Meanwhile, the supplier had invested enormous effort in achieving BS5750. This was seen as being of low importance to most customers. This framework was used by the supplier to reduce effort on 'over achieving/low importance' areas and to focus on 'under achieving/high importance' areas.

Importance/rating reports should also be viewed across accounts and overtime. Two accounts/groups of customers

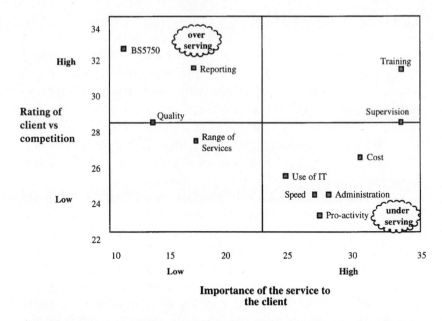

Figure 5.2   Identifying areas for improvement in customer satisfaction: importance vs rating for a temporary staff supplier.

can have significantly differing needs. These differences should be fully recognized by the front-line staff.

Beware of satisfied customers

A simple rating of customer satisfaction might not be enough. Ideally, the research should be asking customers about their intention to purchase in the future. After all, a supplier can do a good job, but the competition might be doing better.

AT&T discovered this problem in the early 1990s. Despite having customer satisfaction surveys that said 95 per cent of customers were satisfied, AT&T was losing sales. Competitors were poaching customers who were satisfied with AT&T but who wanted even more.

The temporary staff supplier experienced a similar problem. Overall, it was rated significantly better than the competition, but detailed analysis showed the areas where competitors had a perceived advantage. For example, a new firm had better scores regarding the 'use of IT'. It emerged that the competitor had developed an 'on-line' linkage with its customers and was using a snazzy presentation package. The supplier closed the gap just in time. A major client was being courted by the competitor on the basis of its use of 'leading edge' technology.

Harness front-line intelligence

The front-line should be the 'eyes and ears' of the supplier but many staff are blind and deaf. The supplier must ensure that front-line staff are alert to customer comments and that there are effective communication lines back to the centre.

Asda is a good role model with its 'tell Archie' scheme. Every member of staff is encouraged to listen to customer comments for issues, ideas and opportunities. Staff then send a yellow note to Archie Norman, the CEO. He is under no obligation to reply (so the system does not become bureaucratic) but the staff member is confident that the information will be read and used to achieve a positive result. The system is simple, avoids bureaucracy and is focused on delivering an action which will improve overall customer service.

Action

Satisfaction surveys, research, etc can all prove invaluable. However, some organizations have become obsessed with blitzing customers with surveys without considering how the information will be converted into positive action. A number of restaurant chains distribute standard customer satisfaction surveys and continue to offer a mediocre service.

It is critical that an organization responds to customer intelligence and to customer complaints. Terry Green, the CEO of Debenhams has the right approach:

> we continually track customer satisfaction versus our direct and indirect competitors. If we see an issue or opportunity we respond immediately. If I receive a customer complaint I treat

it as free consulting advice and ensure that we make the improvements

If a supplier fails to respond to its customers' requirements it is usually because of a negative attitude or a shortage of money. Yet, if the core customers account for 50 per cent of company profits, it is dangerous to ignore their needs. Worse still, poor responsiveness by management can result in the front-line and the customer 'switching off', ie not bothering to feed back to the management. After all, 'if nothing is going to be done, don't do anything.' This attitude can result in a supplier offering worse service until the customer finally disappears.

This was the experience of the British Railways telephone enquiry service. Customers phoned up and were left waiting for ages before the telephone line cut off. These customers complained to British Rail, but no improvement was made. British Rail employees have given up telling their management that there is a problem because nothing gets done. Consequently, there is no positive action and the frustrated customer decided to either fly or drive to the destination.

ELEVATE THE SUPPLIER'S STATUS

The supplier should elevate its status with core customers. It should attempt to move up from 'available supplier' to an 'approved supplier', to 'preferred supplier' to a partner. How is elevation achieved? An increasing proportion of buyers are formally evaluating their suppliers, and telling a vendor where it stands and how it can do better. The supplier can increase its status by achieving the customer's requirements in terms of competency, compliance, consistency, commitment and costs. Even with this explicit information, some suppliers are obtuse. A salesperson might feedback customer complaints but fail to explain how to move up the supplier hierarchy. The benefits of elevation are that the customer is less likely to terminate the business and the supplier will obtain a more intimate understanding of customer needs (see Figure 5.3). This understanding should prove invaluable in securing future business.

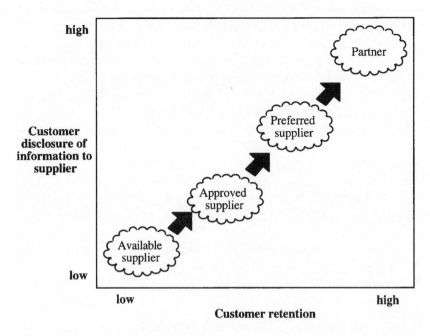

Figure 5.3 Elevating the relationship: the supplier hierarchy.

If the customer is not formally setting the basis for the relationship, the supplier has the scope to impress. First ask: 'how important is the customer to us and how important are we to the customer?' A core profit account is very important to the supplier's bottom line, but can the customer obtain a similar product/service from another vendor? Could it switch supplier at little risk? How much would its bottom line suffer if the supplier refused to supply? If the mutual dependency is high (ie both firms have a lot to lose if the relationship does not work), the benefits of partnership to both sides will be obvious. Intel/Compaq, Marks and Spencer/Northern Foods and Eurotunnel/Eurostar are partnerships which are forged from mutual dependency. However, when the supplier is dependent upon the customer, but the customer can go elsewhere, the supplier must work even harder to elevate and strengthen the relationship.

Moving from an available supplier to being a preferred supplier/partner is not easy but a number of suppliers have found routes to strengthen the relationship. Take, for example, the Shell Petrol Card. As petrol became a commodity and retail availability increased, Shell recognized that customers would switch to competitors. Through introducing its petrol card, it was able to target large fleet operators by providing central invoicing, fleet management services and corporate discounts. This increased the value of the relationship to core profit customers. Shell managed to elevate itself from being just another petrol retailer to being the preferred supplier.

Wrangler, the jeans manufacturer, also found a way of forging partnerships. It has worked with key retailers to improve supply chain efficiency. At one major retailer it transpired that:

▓ lost sales were significant – up to 30 per cent of stock-keeping units (sizes, colours, etc) were off sale at any point in time. This created a sales opportunity of around 6 per cent;

▓ the retailer was overstocked with lines which were not selling. This increased stockholding costs and mark-downs;

▓ a pair of jeans could be manufactured in ten minutes, but half a year separated the cloth being brought into the jeans factory and the finished jeans being purchased by the retailers' customers.

Through introducing EDI link-ups and an improved stock planning system, supply chain costs were reduced while sales increased. Profits for the store were increased by 50 per cent and Wrangler sales were boosted. This cooperation and mutual benefit elevated the status of Wrangler to its retail partners. By consciously upgrading the service Shell and Wrangler have elevated their relationships from the buying office to the customer boardroom.

BOND THE CUSTOMER TO THE SUPPLIER ORGANIZATION

Suppliers often have weak linkages with customers (see Figure 5.4). This is usually appreciated when sales executives leave and take the best customers with them.

The ability to forge a strong bond with customers will vary according to the size and complexity of the business. A rule of thumb is that a supplier should have at least three, strong linkages with a customer. The linkages cannot duplicate effort. Customers do not want to be deluged with three salespeople instead of one and suppliers cannot justify the investment. So how can the bond be strengthened?

Multi-link

First, the sales representative must be tasked to network with at least three decision makers within the customer. The sales representative must also keep detailed, core customer information which is stored on the supplier's premises rather than in his or her head. Any supplier that allows the customer's

TYPICAL LINKAGE

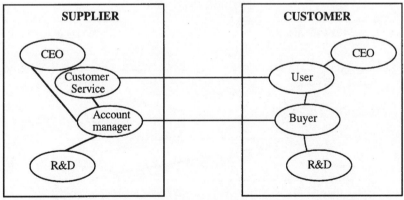

Figure 5.4   Linkages in a typical supplier/customer relationship.

information to walk out the door with the sales executive deserves to go out of business.

The second bond should be 'director to director'. If the customer is producing a significant proportion of the supplier's profits, it warrants the managing director/a senior manager becoming actively involved with the key decision maker within the customer. Whether this takes the form of a regular joint strategy meeting, a lunch or a game of golf, the senior relationship immediately becomes the prime relationship.

The third bond is ideally expert to expert. R&D to R&D or finance to finance can usually provide a strong linkage which can facilitate supplier/customer knowledge. This bonding process can ultimately evolve into a team selling structure. In the team, all members of staff are playing a part in forging the relationship with the customer. This multi-faceted approach ensures that the supplier has plenty of linkages through which it can increase its understanding of customer needs and strengthen the bond (see Figure 5.5).

Such intimacy allows the supplier to be more responsive. It also ensures that the customer belongs to the supplier organization rather than the sales person. The downside is that the interface becomes more complex and the sales person is

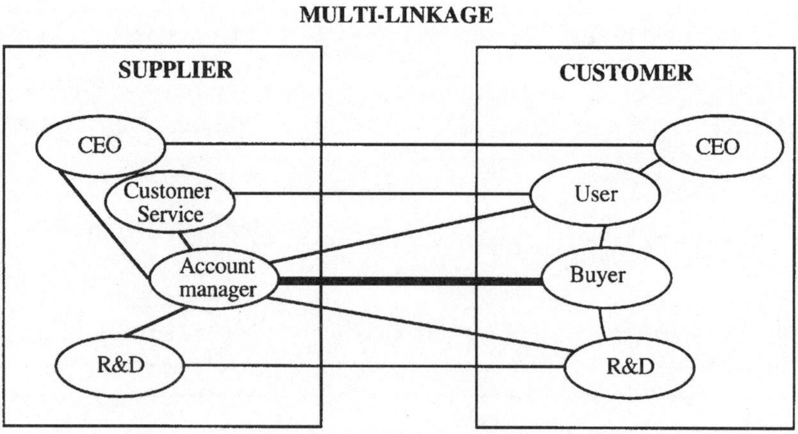

MULTI-LINKAGE

Figure 5.5 Multi-linked supplier/customer relationship.

required to monitor all the communication linkages. But the payback is high. Through the multi-linkages and enhanced intelligence, the supplier benefits from increased customer retention and higher sales. Even a business with low levels of selling resource can benefit from multi-linked relationships. Take Marks and Spencer. Traditionally, shoppers had a limited relationship with M&S. They visited the local store when they wanted to make a purchase and saw the windows from the high street. In the 1980s M&S introduced the M&S store card. This allowed M&S to send frequent mailings to card holders. Card holders are invited to preview evenings where they can be shown new ranges and are sent brochures which detail the new styles. The cardholder information is also used to develop new services for the customer including the launch of the M&S financial services business. The card has changed the nature of the M&S/customer relationship. Rather than there just being the link between store and customer, there is now a direct link to the customer's home. A measure of the success is that M&S has more than 4.5 million cardholders who spent more than £1.5 billion with the firm.

Customer groups

Customer groups and user groups can also strengthen the customer/vendor relationship. This has been used to greatest effect in the computer software industry. Customers are often encouraged to join user groups which meet at conferences and communicate via the Internet. Users help each other resolve problems and adapt the technology to new applications. The groups also serve as a source of information for new product development and product/service refinements.

To date user groups have primarily been used in business-to-business selling. However, they are equally applicable to consumer markets. This has been shown in the US with General Motors' launch of the Saturn car. Owners are encouraged to come along to Saturn events such as barbeques and sports events. By generating a 'club' feel to car ownership, Saturn has strengthened its bond to the customer and has provided the perfect opportunity for dealers to forge a long-term relationship with customers.

Building a strong club/user group is not only the preserve of large companies. Take, for example, Merlin Stickers. The business was started in 1990 and by 1995 had grown to be worth more than £50 million. It produces football stickers which children collect and stick into an album. The price for a packet of six stickers is only 22 pence. Merlin developed the 'swap shop' where collectors meet to swap surplus stickers. The success of this scheme has been amazing. When the swap shop went to Newcastle upon Tyne in 1995 more than 15,000 children turned up. The collectors eagerly swapped and talked about their stickers for the whole day. The swap shops are conducted all over the country. They build sales and have turned sticker collecting into a national occupation for boys aged 8–15.

The need for a strong, multi-faceted linkage with core profit customers is essential in defending the majority of a supplier's future value. Whether via direct communication, user groups or the telephone/Internet, suppliers must work on strengthening the customer bond.

PREPARE FOR FUTURE CUSTOMER NEEDS

Suppliers can be obsessed with satisfying current customer needs but fail to consider future requirements. Yet the majority of a customer's DCP resides in the future rather than the present.

Think about the core customer of the future

Marketing, sales and R&D must continually consider where the customer is likely to be and what it will want in five years' time. This can most easily be achieved by having an internal strategy meeting which focuses on future core customer needs:

░ What will the customers' customers be doing in five years?

░ Will the customer still be purchasing?

▦ Will the supplier's services be more or less valuable to the customer in the future?

▦ What are the major threats to the supplier customer relationship (ie new competitor, substitution of business)?

▦ What are the prime motivators which will change (ie product range, price, service)?

▦ What improvements can the supplier make to the customer relationship?

▦ Are there any pioneering suppliers in other parts of the world which are doing a better job of serving the customer? If so, what is their advantage?

▦ How can technology/new interface systems be employed to reduce costs and improve customer service?

▦ Who will be the key decision makers within the customer in five years and does the supplier have a good relationship with them?

▦ What is the target sales, income and costs-to-serve associated with the customer/customer group over the next five years?

▦ What does the supplier need to do tomorrow to be ready for five years' time?

Having top lined the future agenda, the supplier and some core customers should get together to 'future brainstorm'. The supplier should not be surprised if the customer has not thought much about the future. After all, how many customers in 1985 would have said that they wanted satellite TV, an EDI linkage, a mobile phone or BS5750? It is the supplier's responsibility to give the customer what they want today and be in a position to satisfy their needs of tomorrow.

Involve customers in R&D

Involving customers in future planning also improves product and service developments. For example, experts from British

Airways and United Airlines worked alongside the Boeing engineers when they were developing the 777. This cooperation allowed problems to be resolved at the design stage rather than requiring costly improvements once the plane was operational. The airline partners ensured that the 777 would be cost-effective to operate. They also spotted small points of detail which might have been unnoticed by Boeing. For example, British Airways cabin crew had noticed passengers were alarmed by the falling down of a toilet seat because it sounded like a bomb. Boeing were able to rectify the problem at the design stage rather than incurring costs later in development. Partly due to this enhanced customer intelligence the Boeing 777 achieved a successful launch in 1995.

Similarly, prior to the launch of Windows 95 Microsoft distributed a 'preview program' to over 400,000 expert customers. This extensive final test program allowed Microsoft to identify and rectify bugs prior to the launch of Windows 95. It also meant that 400,000 of the most influential computer operators in the world had a commitment to ensuring that the new product would be a success. This minimized the risks of negative PR and meant that many corporations had a Windows 95 expert prior to the roll-out of the finished product.

Another example of actively involving customers in product development is Intuit, the manufacturer of Quicken (the popular accountancy software package). Intuit requires that all R&D staff spend at least four hours a month listening to the customer service hotline. Through hearing real customers explaining real problems Intuit ensures that all product development staff have a close affinity to real customer needs. This has allowed Intuit to continue developing products which are more relevant and user friendly than competitor systems.

Some R&D directors shy away from such a close proximity to customers. New product development is often conducted in secret with the minimum of involvement from core customers and front-line staff. Yet harnessing the expertise of core customers is increasingly important. The costs of product development are escalating and the margin for error is tightening. Capturing the intelligence from core customers and the front line is essential in reducing the risk of a new initiative failing whilst accelerating product development time.

MANAGE CORE CUSTOMERS THAT ARE IN DECLINE

Core customers are contributing the bulk of a supplier's profits. If they start to decline they will have a profound impact on the bottom line. It is usually easier to recover an account in decline than when it has already terminated business. To know whether a customer is in decline, the supplier needs to have predicted the level of sales and profits that the customer should have produced. This demonstrates the importance of having a good understanding of customer DCP and accurate key account plans. Core customers which are more than 20 per cent below plan should be targeted.

Spot the problem

First, find out what is going on. A customer satisfaction survey, telephone call or a review meeting will explain the situation (the customer does not need to know the reason for the survey). Is the decline due to factors over which the supplier has control or is it due to an external variable? Externals might include the customer dying, having a reduced budget, closing down or no longer requiring the supplier's type of product. If the business has been lost due to controllable factors (ie the product does not satisfy the customer's requirements, it was too expensive, the service was poor, or a competitor could do a better job) the supplier should have a meeting of sales, R&D, product management and anybody else who can help address the problem.

Make a response

Often a customer only requires a gentle reminder or small incentive to return to 'normal behaviour'. Take, for example, the home delivery of newspapers. Home delivery has been in long-term decline. The decline is partly due to uncontrolled factors (readers no longer want a morning paper, have moved house, or the retailer has stopped the delivery service). However, a high proportion of the decline is because the papers are delivered late or because readers have not been reminded to reorder. The danger to the publisher is that when a reader stops home delivery purchase frequency falls. Rather than buying six copies they typically buy four. Even worse, the reader can lose the newspaper buying habit altogether and their purchasing can fall to just one or two copies per week. Through targeting people who move house the publisher ensures that the reader receives delivery to the new home before the habit is lost. It also provides retailers (who undertake home delivery on behalf of the publisher) with incentives to reactivate lapsed customers. Moreover, if any retailer stops home delivery publishers encourage another retailer to take over the 'paper round'. Through introducing these mechanisms, 30 per cent of home delivery terminations can be avoided.

A core customer usually changes his or her behaviour because they have received poor service from the traditional supplier. After all, the majority of customers are more likely to reduce their expenditure than go to the trouble of complaining. The supplier needs to understand what has happened prior to rebuilding the relationship. Take, for example, a small shirt laundry business in South London. It collects dirty shirts from offices in the City and returns them 24 hours later laundered and pressed. Like many small firms, it experienced 'growth pains' when it expanded and took on new deliverers. The new deliverers tended to be less punctual and polite than the 'old boys'. Some customers were unhappy and stopped using the service. The owner spotted that the sales were down from some loyal customers (which were worth £200 pa). He phoned each of the customers up, learnt of the problems, apologized profusely, changed the delivery arrangements and offered each customer three free laundered shirts. All the customers were recovered and the business resumed its expansion plans.

ENCOURAGE LOYALTY

If a supplier is surpassing customer expectations, has a 'preferred'/'partner' status, with a strong customer bond, is prepared for the future and is carefully managing those customers which are in decline, it might not need to worry about encouraging customer loyalty. However, customers increasingly expect to be rewarded for the business they place with a supplier. Moreover, loyalty schemes can produce incremental profits, prove a useful defence mechanism against competitor activity and an invaluable source of competitive intelligence. These benefits need to be offset against the costs of operating such a scheme. After all, loyalty schemes can prove expensive but their real value can be difficult to prove.

Successful loyalty programmes include the American Airlines frequent flyer scheme. This was the first frequent flyer programme in the airline industry. At the time the airline industry had been deregulated and new competition was sprouting up on all the profitable routes. Prices on the main routes were squeezed and American Airlines appeared disadvantaged due to its enormous scale and large infrastructure. Bob Crandall, the American Airlines CEO, devised the frequent flyer programme as a mechanism to exploit the airline's scale. It encouraged flyers to consolidate all their miles on American, even if they could buy a cheaper individual ticket from one of the smaller carriers.

The scheme was particularly popular with the most profitable type of passenger, the business flyer. Business men and women tended to specify when, where and with which airline they wanted to fly, but their employers picked up the bill. These flyers eagerly joined the American scheme, as the free miles could be used for personal trips. The scheme was particularly effective because the perceived value of the free travel was high even if the actual cost was comparatively low. For example, a frequent flyer might perceive the price of a return economy flight between New York and London as being £600. However, the marginal cost of flying the extra frequent flyer could be under £150. The scheme proved very successful. American prospered while many of the start-ups failed.

Several ingredients are required to produce a successful loyalty scheme.

▨ ***High perceived value at low cost.*** A loyalty scheme would typically cost a supplier no more than 2 per cent of turnover. The supplier must, therefore, find a reward which has a high perceived value but a low actual cost. Air travel and hotel rooms balance this equation due to their favourable marginal economics. Enhanced customer service can also work. For example, Debenhams (the largest department store chain in the UK) offers customers who spend more than £500 pa 'Gold card service'. This includes a special lounge, free coffee, invites to events and free parking. The actual costs of the service enhancements are relatively low yet the perceived value is high. Meanwhile, other retailers offered customers who spent £500 the opportunity to get 15 per cent off future purchases. Such schemes proved too expensive and had to be redesigned.

Relevance. Free air travel from airlines makes sense but there have been some strikingly inappropriate loyalty schemes. Buy a newspaper for a year and receive a reduced price television set and eat 10 meals at an Italian restaurant chain and receive a ticket to Paris are notable for their inconsistency with the core proposition.

Choice. If a reward is to be valued by the customer it should offer some degree of choice. Auto drivers can quickly tire of free glasses and video tapes. Hence the success of the Texaco loyalty scheme. Through offering points which could be redeemed against a wide range of products, it achieved an enrolment around 50 per cent above a traditional petrol loyalty scheme.

Convenience. A loyalty reward should be simple for the customer to use. If receipts need to be returned, complex forms completed and other obstacles overcome the scheme is likely to fail. The Profiles system operated by Visa is a good example of the simplicity required. The Visa customer fills in a simple form and is credited with one point when he or she spends £10. The points are automatically calculated by Visa and the customer is notified of the accumulated points on each statement. Having accumulated sufficient points, the customer can order a gift from the Profiles catalogue. The scheme is easy to understand and the only requirement placed on the customer is that they make their spend on Visa. All other obstacles and hurdles have been removed.

Advance notice. A supplier should tell all customers of the benefits of being loyal. This advance notice will ensure that new recruits appreciate the benefits of hanging around. A good example is the insurance industry. Car owners know that their insurance 'no claims bonus' increases over time.

Accountability. The real costs and profitability of a loyalty scheme must be tightly controlled. Set-up, administration and reward expenses need to be fully costed and clear targets are required to measure the incremental profit that the scheme produces.

Information. A loyalty scheme should provide unparalleled customer intelligence. Through monitoring customer behaviour in relation to the incentives offered, the supplier will be able to constantly refine the programme.

In the mid-1990s there have been a flood of loyalty schemes. The most successful launch in the UK has been the Tesco Club Card. It is simple for the customer to use, supports the core Tesco proposition and has been precisely targeted and costed. It shows virtually all the ingredients of a successful loyalty scheme:

High perceived value: the club member receives a £2.50 voucher for every £250 they spend. There are also special offers. For example, spend £400 in the run up to Christmas and receive a free turkey.

Relevance: the club motto is 'every little helps'. This endorses the practical, value-conscious philosophy of Tesco.

Choice: the vouchers can be used anywhere in a Tesco store at any time. A typical Tesco store has more than 30,000 lines offering plenty of customer choice.

Convenience: the shopper can complete the simple enrolment form at the checkout and instantly receive the plastic membership card. The card is used to monitor the spend and 'voucher points' accumulated by the member. At the end of each quarter Tesco sends the member his or her vouchers. All the customer is required to do is enrol and spend more than £10 per visit to Tesco.

▦ *Notice:* all existing and prospective customers have been told of the benefits of the scheme through store, staff and press communications.

▦ *Accountability:* Tesco has been very clear in the targets that have been set for the card. The programme is designed to increase the frequency of purchase by certain customer groups and to build average transaction values. Moreover, tesco has incentivized club members to consolidate all their grocery spend at the score.

▦ *Information:* Tesco are now able to monitor the time of spend and level of spend by different customer groups. They can also see the products bought and the sensitivity to price. This provides Tesco with an unparalleled source of customer intelligence which allows product ranges and promotional activity to be constantly refined.

The Tesco scheme had one further advantage: it was the first to be offered by a UK grocer. This first-mover advantage has made it very difficult for competitors to put forward a better scheme. This helped prompt more than 4.5 million customers to enrol in the first six months of operation. The success of Tesco has subsequently been copied by other retailers in the UK. By 1998 Sainsbury, Boots and WH Smith and more than 30 other retailers introduced club schemes. In fact more than 50 per cent of the population now use retail club or loyalty scheme. As such, it is more difficult to drive incremental profits from the club programme.

In 1995 the Halifax Building Society, Britain's largest mortgage supplier, also started to reward loyal customers by providing them with more favourable mortgages than new customers. This was a fundamental change within the financial services business. Historically, lenders would compete to offer new customers the most attractive deal while 'milking' loyal customers. This encouraged customers to shop around and smart home owners would remortgage their properties. The Halifax has now taken a deliberate step to reward loyal and long-standing customers and to lock them in.

Although there have been many successful loyalty schemes, suppliers need to be careful when they start giving money back to core profit customers. The plan can be very noble and should enhance customer retention, but it can leave a hole in the bottom line. A number of major airlines have been forced to review and even terminate their frequent flyer programmes as the liability for free flights has grown. Not only can an out-of-control loyalty system threaten the bottom line, it can also upset the most valuable customers if it is terminated prematurely. These potential downsides must force a supplier to develop a scheme with due care. It is also worth remembering that if the supplier has not offered a reward in the past, it does not need to offer an all singing and dancing loyal scheme from the start. Instead, it can slowly increase the benefits that are offered to loyal customers. This minimizes the profit risk and allows the supplier to add more value later in the relationship.

NEVER BELIEVE THAT A CORE CUSTOMER IS SAFE

It is easy to take loyal, profitable customers for granted. They do not generate the corporate attention that surrounds a new recruit or a complaining customer. But if a customer is particularly valuable to a supplier, a competitor will spot the attractiveness and will attempt to poach it. Suppliers need to be constantly on their guard.

Beware the quiet ones

Following a car accident the person that shouts loudest is often the fittest while the quietest person can be on the critical list. The same rule applies to customer management. The majority of customers do not bother to complain – they just switch their business without making a fuss. No news is often bad news. It is therefore in the supplier's interest to preserve regular dialogue with core profit customers.

Make it easy to complain

A complaining customer is better than no customer at all. The mechanism must be available when the customer wants to make the move (eg a 24-hour hotline), it must respond quickly, it must be easy to use and it must guarantee a response. Often it pays to empower front-line staff to deal with the issue immediately. For example, B & Q, the UK homecare retailer, will allow checkout staff to make refunds of up to £15 on the spot with no need to consult a manager. The complaints process is effective, friendly, fast, minimizes administration costs and encourages staff to act responsibly.

Give a little bit more

Much has been written about delighting and 'wowing' customers. Yet it is difficult to wow customers year after year. It is possible to keep giving them a bit more. This effort to constantly improve product and service gives the customer better value and ensures that front-line divisions are continually thinking about the needs of core profit customers.

A good example of this philosophy can be seen at the Daily Mail. In 1980 the *Daily Mail* was a black and white newspaper, it had no supplements, carried few special offers and contained 48 pages. At the time it was considered 'excellent value' by its readers. By continually thinking about reader requirements the paper has added value which has improved the reader experience. Today the editorial content has been refined, the paper is full of colour, it carries exciting offers, special supplements and has 60 pages. The Daily Mail's market share has increased and even more customers perceive the paper as being 'excellent'.

Adding value to core customers can prove expensive and a supplier might feel that the costs cannot be justified. However, this investment should be considered in terms of the incremental sales/margins that are produced and the benefits of increased customer retention. The supplier should also ask whether increased benefits can be funded by cutting unnecessary services to core customers. For example, credit cards can continue to send magazines to members even when the majority are unread. Sales and service staff can call when they are not required. Stores can operate promotional events which only attract 2 per cent of core customers and restaurants can continue handing out 'customer satisfaction forms' even though the information is not used. Through constantly attempting to give the customer a bit more, while cutting out unnecessary services, the supplier can strengthen the bond with customers without increasing costs.

Acute suppliers must constantly review the degree to which core profit customers are 'locked in'. Through surpassing customer expectations, elevating the relationship, strengthening the bond, preparing for the future, managing the decline, rewarding loyalty and never taking them for granted the supplier should retain and develop core customers. This series of 'lock-ins' will defend the profit base and will create a real barrier to block out competitive threat. The supplier can then confidently develop the new profit streams.

6

INCREASING INCOME

The routes to increased income are many and elusive. Millions of CEOs, marketing staff, sales executives, advertising agencies and consultants are constantly finding new and creative ways to increase income. The enormous array of development activities can be broadly classified into five routes (see Figure 6.1). Some of these routes might be termed 'strategic' while others are 'tactical'. Some can have a short-term impact on profits while others could involve a long-term repositioning.

No route to profit is straightforward. Just as the realignment of prices can have a long-term impact on customer recruitment, so the selling of new services can affect pricing structures. Despite the interrelation of variables it is useful to review each path individually. First review the opportunities to build sales and then consider opportunities to raise margins.

EXISTING SERVICES TO EXISTING CLIENTS

Can a supplier sell more of what it currently produces to existing customers? The immediate reaction of most sales executives is that the customer is already 'fully loaded' but is this really the case? In order to optimize sales the supplier must:

- evaluate the depth of the customer's pocket;
- evaluate the routes to increase the share of the pocket;
- reach all the customer decision-makers;

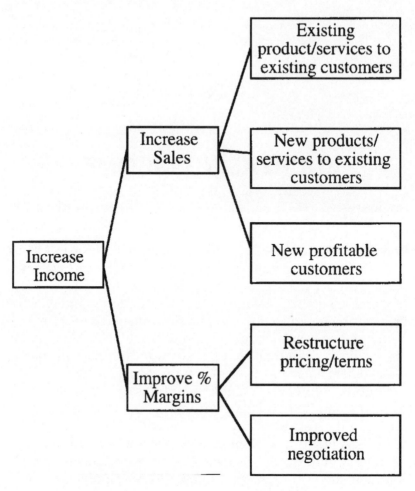

Figure 6.1   Routes to increasing income.

▨ ensure that the 'back-up' is in place;

▨ accelerate the time taken to get new product developments to the customer/improve customer retention.

Optimize the share of the customer's pocket

How much does the customer spend on products/services
which the supplier could supply? Many firms do not even ask

this question and the majority of salespeople get the answer wrong. A salesperson might estimate the opportunity to be last year's sales and a bit more, but what about the rest?

How much does the customer spend with competitors?

Does the customer have related departments, divisions or subsidiaries which buy from a different source?

Is the customer making a spend which could be substituted for the supplier's products and services?

Take, for example, a specialist packaging firm which supplies a global chemical organization. When asked about the size of the pocket, the account manager estimated it to be £300,000 (of which the supplier had £200,000). A detailed evaluation of the customer showed the account manager was looking at the tip of the iceberg. The actual value of the pocket was closer to £1.5 million (Figure 6.2).

Having checked the whereabouts of the opportunity, the supplier was able to identify the obstacles to achieving the business. In some cases it needed to access new corners of the customer's empire. Other opportunities required investment in new packaging designs and expertise in the local market. The supplier systematically reviewed the parts of the business which

Area of sales opportunity	£000s
Initial estimate of depth of pocket	300
Competitors sales to customer	200
Divisions not covered by the supplier (ie Agriculture, Medical and Industrials)	350
Markets not covered by the supplier (ie US, Latin America, Japan)	600
Total depth of pocket	**1450**

Figure 6.2 Example of the depth of the customer's pocket: the packaging industry.

were easiest and most profitable to secure. It identified and overcame the various obstacles and was able to increase its sales from £200,000 to £650,000 in three years. Not only did this increase profits, but it ensured that the supplier was more secure when the customer started to cut its supplier base.

If a supplier has a large number of customers it can prove impossible to examine the depth of pocket for every account. A shortcut is to examine the frequency of purchase and the average transaction value for the customer base and then to profile individual accounts/customer groups against the norm. Figure 6.3 shows the frequency of purchase versus the average transaction value for a chain of supermarkets. It transpired that 22 per cent of customers visited an outlet frequently and had a high transaction value. This group of 'core customers' were producing 44 per cent of sales and needed to be defended against competitive manoeuvres. Meanwhile, 23 per cent of customers visited the chain infrequently but had a high transaction value. The supermarket planned how these customers could be encouraged to come in more often by offering repeat visit incentives.

Conversely, 10 per cent of customers visited frequently but had a low transaction value. The chain reviewed how the spend per visit could be increased. In some cases there was little opportunity to increase spend. The elderly and unemployed visited frequently but had only shallow pockets. Yet within the frequent low spenders there were groups which could be encouraged to spend more. 'Impulse lines' at the checkout triggered incremental spend from certain types of customer. Meanwhile incentives to buy more also stimulated purchasing.

It is easiest to increase the purchase frequency of 'infrequents' or the transaction value of 'low spenders'. Attempting to change the behaviour of an 'infrequent low spender' tends to be more difficult. This philosophy of developing the frequency and transaction value of individual customers/customer groups works in the retail environment and is even more appropriate in business-to-business selling. The first requirement is for the manager to understand why a customer/group of customers performs differently than the 'norm'. Some behaviour is inherent

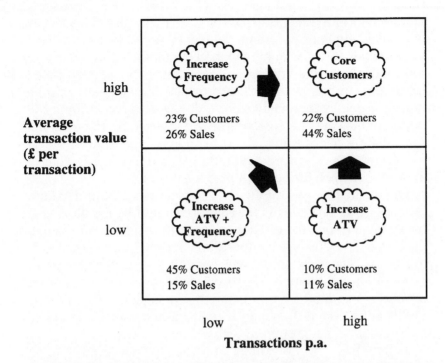

Figure 6.3 Example of transaction frequency and transaction value profile: customers for a UK grocery retailer.

and there is little opportunity for the supplier to increase profitable sales. However, there are usually opportunities to increase the frequency or value of spend. For example:

Stay in touch

A thank you letter for the business placed, regular mailings and customer meetings can all stimulate additional purchases. Take the mail-order catalogue business. 'Hot mailings' are sent to those customers which have recently placed an order offering a special incentive to order again. Hot mailings usually achieve a 10 per cent hit rate because a customer that has recently ordered is more likely to order again.

Cover the decision makers

It is critical that the supplier covers all the decision makers if it is to close the sale. The scale of the missed opportunity is illustrated by some recent work for a leading global speciality chemicals supplier. Of eight people responsible for the customer's 'buy decision', only two had contact with the sales representative from the supplier. Consequently, the supplier failed to obtain a full understanding of the customer need. Despite having a long-term relationship, the sale was lost. During the period of the sale, the customer was contacted by 13 personnel from the supplier's service and technical departments. These personnel were unaware that there was a major sales initiative in progress which further confused the customer.

The ability to cover all the decision makers and understand all the customer needs is best demonstrated by the Japanese heavy engineering firms. They will usually send a business delegation to the customer rather than despatching a small selling team. The delegation will include key staff from R&D, production and finance. These will plug into all the customer requirements. Moreover, because the delegation can see any problem first hand, they can usually 'bottom out' issues prior to completing an agreement with the customer.

Meanwhile, US and European firms typically send a small selling team. This individual/group is not able to cover all the decision makers and can miss issues. Furthermore, the Western sales executive will probably be busy sending faxes back to head office to get problems resolved. The people at head office do not see the issues first hand, consequently more time is spent detailing the situation and communication breakdowns can occur.

Stimulate repurchasing

A customer of Viking Direct, the mail-order office supplies firm, will receive over 40 catalogues, special promotion catalogues and newsletters each year. These come with different incentives to order. This dynamic and innovative way of presenting office supplies has increased transaction frequency. Similarly McDonald's has constructed an elaborate promotional programme which is designed to increase customer traffic at the quiet times of the year. Special offers, children's collections and competitions rotate to create interest and a reason to visit.

Trade up customers

The old retail tactics of 'spend £100 and get £5 off' and 'buy two get one free' are crude reflections of the strategy. Richer Sounds, the British hi-fi retailer, increases transaction values through excellent salesmanship. Through a combination of friendliness, impeccable service, product authority and sales confidence Richer Sounds staff comfortably 'trade customers up'. A customer might plan to spend £150 on a CD player but will probably come out better informed, with a superior product costing £200. This has helped Richer Sounds achieve the highest sales and profit per square foot of any UK retailer, while achieving extraordinarily high levels of customer satisfaction.

Accelerate the speed of getting to market

Much has been written about shortening product lifecycles and the need to get to market quickly. This need places increased pressure on the front line at the time of a new product launch. As the costs of advertising and new product development inflate, the need to secure a 'rapid fire' distribution is intensified.

Microsoft has set a new world standard for getting to the market. In order to maximize global hype, while minimizing the risks of grey marketing, Microsoft adopted a 'Big Bang' approach to launch Windows 95. This tested the front line as follows:

- retail distribution was synchronized to match the enormous barrage of advertising/PR;
- over 1600 fully trained customer service staff dealt with the hundreds of thousands of enquiries that were received in the first few days of the launch;
- troubleshooters quickly resolved any product or service problems.

The result was the most successful launch/product upgrade of all time:

▦ virtually 100 per cent availability was achieved on the first day of launch in most Western markets;

▦ potential buyers could review Windows 95 on the Internet on the day of launch;

▦ relatively little negative PR was produced despite competitors and newspapers wanting to talk up any problems;

▦ seven million copies were sold in the first two months of the launch;

▦ nine out of ten customers were satisfied and claimed that they would purchase again.

Microsoft has set the standard by which other product launches will be compared. Most new product launches compare unfavourably. For example, a recent over-the-counter drug from a major pharmaceuticals manufacturer took four months to achieve full market availability because the salesforce were targeted to support 23 other products. Meanwhile an adhesive used in the plastics industry took eight months to reach all prospective buyers because the company had only three sales representatives covering the whole of Europe. In a world where new products are lucky if they are famous for 15 minutes, a slow roll out is unacceptable.

Back-up in place

Having targeted the pocket, identified the obstacles and covered the decision makers, the sale can still be lost. Some suppliers throw the business away because they fail to back up the front line. R&D might be slow to assemble the product redesigns, service might fail to guarantee the installation or finance might be slow in putting the numbers together. In a retail outlet the right stock-keeping unit might be missing or there is a queue at the till. It is critical that all divisions are supporting the front line in selling to the customer.

Systematically marshall the selling resource

The opportunity to systematically grow sales by improving coverage, order frequency and transaction values was reflected at a

UK convenience foods manufacturer (see Figure 6.4). It discovered that the sales activity was missing around 10 per cent of the key outlets within the market. By covering these decision makers overall sales were increased by 3 per cent. Moreover, the average order value could be increased by adjusting the trade pricing structures to encourage retailers to take extra product flavours while reducing 'out-of-stocks'. The combined benefit of this activity increased sales by 4 per cent. Finally, the supplier increased order frequency by working with retailers to improve the presentation of the product, while enhancing the impact of promotions. This extended the amount of shelf space that the product range could command and accelerated retailer sell-through rates. Retailers ordered more frequently which strengthened the relationship they had with the supplier. This helped build sales by a further 7 per cent. Through outsourcing these

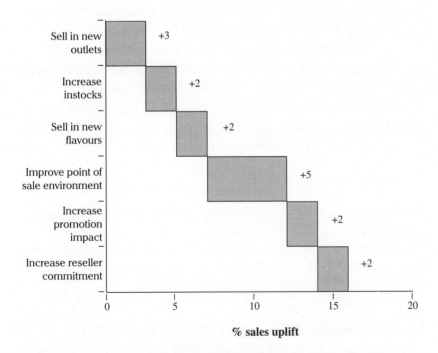

Figure 6.4 Percentage sales uplift achieved by convenience food supplier through focused trade development.

Source: UK convenience food supplier (turnover £70 million)

activities to a specialist field marketing company, which focused effort on each of the opportunity areas, overall sales were increased by 16 per cent whilst selling costs were cut by 18 per cent. This example serves to remind managers that significant additional income can be produced by making the existing customer base work a little harder.

Failure to optimize sales

Failure to optimize the sales from the existing customer base can be due to a number of factors:

▓ Senior management attention may be attracted to more glamorous areas such as investor relations, strategic opportunities for growth and 're-engineering' the organization.

▓ Too many sales directors have come up through the ranks and see themselves as managers of the salesforce rather than being responsible for tapping the incremental profits in the customer base.

▓ Customer service directors can be more concerned about customer service measures rather than considering how they can increase profitable sales to an individual customer.

▓ Marketing staff tend to focus on the opportunities present within the 'market' rather than examining the particular opportunities resident within an individual customer/small groups of customers.

Increasing sales of existing products to existing customers is mundane yet it is the major route to increasing the value of the customer base. Senior management need to permanently review whether sales opportunities are being lost and challenge front-line departments to deliver more.

NEW PRODUCTS/SERVICES TO EXISTING CUSTOMERS

Could the supplier make additional profit by exploiting new parts of the customer's pocket? Could it add value to existing services? Or could it sell entirely new products? After all, many supplier/customer relationships are firmly grounded and have already responded to the changing requirements of both partners. For example:

■ IBM has been supplying the US government for a large part of the twentieth century;

■ hundreds of thousands of *Daily Telegraph* readers have bought the paper regularly since the 1950s;

■ Merrill Lynch have thousands of customers which date back to the 1930s;

■ Beretta has been supplying the various forms of the Italian Army for the last 400 years.

In all these cases the original product which was used to forge the supplier/customer relationship has changed significantly. During the relationship the supplier has developed an unparalleled understanding of individual customer needs and motivations. This intelligence has formed the basis of providing new products and services for the customer.

Let's consider how a customer relationship can be exploited to find new routes to add value to the existing product/service and then consider the scope to develop new products and services. If the supplier has an intimate understanding of the customer's business it might be able to add real value, ie help the account increase profits by reducing its costs or building sales. If a supplier can deliver these benefits, it is in a position to negotiate an improved income. The opportunity to add value to the relationship has been heightened since customers have 'downsized' or focused on 'core competencies'. Customers no longer carry the in-house staff that would have been responsible for adjusting, fitting or fixing the product and increasingly require suppliers to provide the service.

Reducing costs or risk on behalf of the customer

There are a variety of routes by which a supplier can help a customer save money without cutting prices. It can reduce the customer's costs of acquiring, possessing or using a product. Each of these can help add real value to the customer relationship thereby defending supplier margins (see Figure 6.5).

Increase product longevity

Books for Students is one of the largest distributors of books to schools and libraries in the UK. In the 1980s it recognized that library budgets were being cut and schools were increasingly value conscious. BFS designed plastic jackets which protected paperback books which increased their longevity by 40 per cent. Customers could therefore buy paperbacks rather than hardbacks allowing budgets to be stretched further. Customers responded positively to the jackets allowing BFS to charge for the jacketing service. The value advantage allowed BFS to increase its share of the market and boost profitability.

Reduce handling costs

In the 1980s the market for bandages, syringes, etc was under threat from cheap, private label suppliers. A bandage was seen as being a strip of cotton. The sales and marketing people at Johnson & Johnson saw this threat to the traditional market but saw something much more important. In an emergency case the cost of a bandage is insignificant when compared with its real value. An entire operation can be delayed if medical staff are required to assemble the right dressings, bandages, scissors, etc. Johnson & Johnson recognized the importance of product handling in the medical area and developed kits which would contain the dressings and support materials required for a given type of operation. These kits are easy to store, open and use. The kits save time for doctors and nurses which ultimately saves lives. Although a hospital might be spending more on its bandages, it is saving much bigger costs elsewhere in the budget. Johnson & Johnson have successfully saved the customer money while increasing their share of a hospitals 'pocket'.

Customer Cost Area	Cost/Risk	Opportunity for a supplier to help the customer make savings
Acquisition	Cost of goods	Reduce customer wastage/increase product longevity
	Buying cost	Minimize paperwork/buying administration costs
Possession	Storage/ obsolescence	Cut customer inventory
	Interest	Offer favourable interest charges
	Handling	Easy to store and handle
Usage	Direct	Simplest, quickest, cheapest to use
	Indirect production costs	Minimal training, back up, admin. etc
Total		Lowest total cost for customer

Figure 6.5 Routes to reduce total costs for customer.

Source: Based on a framework developed by Frank Cespedes in Concurrent Marketing *(1995).*

Save the customer time

The commercial printing and stationery market is notoriously competitive yet Oyez Stationery has developed a profitable niche. It has developed a particular understanding of the requirements of the legal profession. Oyez has recognized that lawyers cost £150 per hour but spend much of their time wading through documents. By fully investigating the needs of lawyers, they have designed legal forms which are easy to use and save legal staff time. Lawyers pay a premium for Oyez forms when compared with standard commercial stationery, but who would begrudge spending £1 extra on a form if it saves £100 of legal time?

Reduce financing costs

In the automotive and computer markets, the large manufacturers have a lower cost of capital than their customers. They can offer low-cost leasing schemes which allow customers to free up investment spending for other areas.

In these examples, suppliers have developed solutions for groups of customers which add real value, either through reducing the cost of goods, saving administration/production costs or bearing risks on behalf of the customer. This philosophy can be equally applied to an individual customer when it is profitable to do so. For example, in the US, Airbourne Express recognized that Xerox need early morning deliveries so that sales and service staff could get moving early in the day rather than be waiting for parts to be delivered. Airbourne Express rethought its entire distribution arrangements so that it could guarantee the Xerox deliveries at 8.30 am rather than the 10.30 am delivery that was being offered by competitors. This customized service allowed Xerox to improve the productivity of its sales and service operations thereby saving money while improving customer service. Xerox was therefore happy to award its distribution contract to Airbourne Express even if it was more expensive than the 10.30 am service offered by competitors.

Help the customer to increase its sales

Just as a supplier can help the customer save money/minimize long-term liabilities, it might also be able to help it build sales or improve service. For example, Frontline is responsible for distributing magazines to wholesalers and retailers on behalf of several publishers. It distributes 24 per cent of the UK's magazines. Frontline recognized that most independent newsagents are unsophisticated and cannot afford to design the ideal shelf planograms for magazines. It invested in research to construct the ideal magazine range and layout for different types of retail outlet. The planograms improved retail presentation of magazines and sales increased by 12 per cent in participating outlets. This increased the profit for retailers while building Frontline's sales.

A similar philosophy can be seen at Procter and Gamble in the US. In January 1997 the P&G salesforce was re-branded the 'Customer Business Development group'. CBD staff assist customers in optimizing inventory levels, and tailoring promotion plans to the local market. As Tom Muccio, P&G's vice president of customer business development for WalMart commented to Sales and Marketing magazine:

> It's not selling on a transactional basis, it's presenting solutions as part of an overall plan. WalMart wants to exceed customer expectations and so do we. Everything we're doing – from distribution to pricing to merchandising – is trying to focus on the consumer, because we share the consumer.

Introduce new products and services

The supplier might be able to extract more profit from the customer base by selling it something new. For example, in the early 1980s Digital were in the business of selling computer hardware. However, Digital saw that customers were sourcing hardware and software from an increasing number of suppliers and this complexity increased customer problems in terms of getting everything to work. In response to this need, Digital set up 'Multi Vendor Support Services' on behalf of major customers. This business unit would manage the helplines and computer service desks on behalf of individual customers whether the user was having a problem an IBM, Dell or Compaq machine. This business has boomed and is now worth around $5 billion. It is offering a broad array of support services to clients as diverse as the NatWest Bank, Microsoft and small companies which only have a handful of machines. Digital successfully evolved customer relationships into a new, profitable service for the 1990s.

Likewise in 1995 the Prudential, Britain's largest life insurers, announced that it was offering a banking service. The logic is simple. The life insurance industry appears stagnant and new competitors are entering the market. However, the Prudential has a salesforce of 6500 staff who have good relationships with the company's six million long-standing customers. The new banking service will exploit this relationship. Moreover, the Prudential is already paying out hundreds of millions to customers whose insurance policies have matured. Traditionally, these customers would have taken their cheque from the Prudential and might have paid it into a bank. By offering the new service, the Prudential will be able to prolong the relationship and exploit greater value from the customer.

Both Digital and the Prudential have invested the capital required to set up these new services. However, the risks can be offset by partnering with a supplier that has the expertise/product/service but lacks the customers. Take, for example, the airline industry. Alliances between Delta and Virgin and Northwest/KLM increase the penetration of the customer's pocket. Virgin is unlikely to establish a service from New York to Dallas but hundreds of its transatlantic customers will want to make the onward journey. Delta offers a regular service on this route and the alliance between the two companies means the customer can purchase a through ticket. Likewise, Microsoft has linked up with around 7000 'Microsoft solution providers'. These firms have a detailed expertise of certain industry sectors (eg chemicals) or business processes (eg finance). The solution providers help ensure that the software product is tailored to the specific needs of the customer. This improves the value of the software to the client and increases the Microsoft/solution provider 'share of pocket'.

The same philosophy has been adopted by a small newsagent in a village on the outskirts of London. Five years ago it delivered only newspapers to its customers. Demand for home-delivered newspapers was in decline and the service was becoming no longer viable. After a drink in the village pub the newsagent set up a 'partnership' with a local dry cleaner. The newsagent advertises dry-cleaning services, collects and delivers the laundry to the household, and adds the charges to the news bill. The laundry gives the newsagent a 25 per cent discount to cover the cost of the service. The scheme was so successful that the newsagent added shoe repairs, photo-developing and groceries to the service. As a result the newsagent's turnover has doubled, its profits quadrupled and its customer satisfaction has increased. In the meantime at least 5000 village newsagents have closed because their business has become no longer viable.

There are risks associated with diversification. Management can become distracted or customers confused when the portfolio is extended. However, if the extension is a genuine response to the requirements of core customers, and does increase discounted customer profitability, it is usually worth the effort.

ATTRACT NEW PROFITABLE CUSTOMERS

Looking for new customers might appear to contradict the concept of customer base management. After all, a new customer is not even on the customer register. Yet managers must be ever vigilant for the opportunity. First they must question whether they are missing profitable customers. Has a competitor cherry picked the most attractive customers within the market leaving the supplier with the rump? Are there customers which are being ignored by the supplier which will be profitable in the future?

Target the most profitable customers within the existing market

It is useful to model the DCP for competitors. Do they have more attractive customers than your firm? Why is this? What can be done to win them? When this exercise was undertaken by an engineering firm it emerged that the small machine shops which it believed were 'too small to bother with' were producing exceptional levels of profit for a competitor.

Review new markets/channels

Low tariffs, cheap communications and affordable transport have created an unprecedented array of opportunities. Management must free up the energy and resources to explore the opportunities and filter out the routes to profit. It is worth remembering that, despite the current problems, by

2010 the Far East market will be larger and faster growing than either Europe or the United States.

Amid this explosive growth in new markets a supplier is likely to find new, profitable customers. For inspiration managers should look to European Telecom. This firm established its first office in London in 1989 expecting to serve primarily the European market. Soon after its formation it received a chance enquiry from Hong Kong. The CEO bought the cheapest ticket and jetted off to the Far East. He returned with an order for £1 million. By 1995 the firm had grown to reach a turnover of £70 million with a strong profit stream.

International growth can generate huge profits but it brings associated risks of bad debt, a loss of control and distraction to management. The majority of medium-sized firms are poorly equipped to deal with such opportunities. In the UK it appears that only 5 per cent of a typical firm's selling costs are devoted to the export markets which are based outside of Europe. These sales personnel tend to be under-resourced and lack the corporate back-up they require.

Closer to home, a supplier can also miss the emergence of customer groups and trade channels. For example, many of the European insurance companies were slow to develop 'direct' selling systems which cater for the younger, more sophisticated customer. Likewise, some US grocery suppliers were slow to recognize the demise of the 'mom and pop' stores and the growth of the major discounters like Walmart. In both cases the supplier missed the evolution of a new customer base. They were left with sales representatives calling on outlets which had closed while they lacked the depth of key account resources to properly service Walmart.

The message is simple. The existing customer base will generate the majority of profits over the next five years. However, marketing and selling personnel need to scour the home and international marketplace to find the new generation of customers. A formal approach to planning this market coverage is critical, otherwise a lot of effort is wasted attracting the wrong sorts of customer. After all, there is little point in recruiting a customer if it will produce a below average DCP. If an organization is missing profitable customers, it is usually the result of poor targeting or complacency.

Customer targeting

A disciplined approach to identifying and targeting attractive customers has been witnessed at MCI in the US. This large telecommunications group adopted the 'Family and Friends' scheme which entailed MCI asking its customers (who tended to have a high average spend on the telephone) to propose a friend to sign up to MCI. Talkative customers tend to have talk-ative friends hence MCI used a simple approach to attract attractive recruits. Both the existing member and the new cus-tomer shared a discount, allowing MCI to attract profitable new customers while rewarding its core customers.

Having targeted the most profitable recruits the supplier must develop the relationship and close the sale. This requires effective management of all stages in the sales process. The majority of European firms continue to under-manage the cus-tomer recruitment process. Profitable recruits can be missed or given insufficient attention. Take the customer recruitment process at a supplier of corporate credit cards. Historically marketing/sales managers had been targeted according to the sales increase over the previous year's performance. However, in comparison to the market penetration in other regions, one region had managed to lose 376 prospective customers through sloppy management of the recruitment process (see Figure 6.7).

The DCP for a typical new customer was calculated to be £13,000 per customer. Therefore, the Regional Sales Director had failed to capture around £4.9 million of profit relative to other regions, even though the region was outperforming its plan. Having seen the scale of the lost opportunity, the Regional Sales Director set about monitoring, managing and tightening each stage in the recruitment process. This helped reduce the lost prospective customers to below the company average.

A supplier must establish a formal process for measuring and managing each stage of the customer recruitment process. It must also forge a culture in which individuals con-

Stage	Problems in sales region	'Lost prospective customers'	% of loss
Prospects	No focused targeting of attractive customers	215	**57.2%**
Enquiry	Customer enquiries 'lost' due to poor telephone backup/process management	65	**17.3%**
Sell	Sales people lacked clear understanding of customer need	61	**16.3%**
Close	Sales skills/support inappropriate to close the sale	35	**9.3%**
		376	100.0%

Figure 6.6 Measuring and managing customer recruitment: corporate credit card supplier.

tinually strive to improve the identification and closure of attractive prospects. Possibly the receptionist is too slow at answering the phone, the sales assistant might not speak the language of the enquirer, the office might be closed, or maybe the sales executive lacks the expertise to close certain types of customer. Such problems will only become clear when management has the information and performance measures to evaluate each stage of the recruitment process.

Complacency

A sales team can exceed its sales and annual profit targets while still being complacent. How so? Most sales people know that it is easier to push 5 per cent more to 20 existing customers than to win a new account. Left to their own devices sales executives will usually 'over-trawl' existing customers. This year's sales and profits might look great and the sales people will get full bonuses, but the customer base is being eroded. Four years later the firm will lack the breadth of customer base to continue growing sales. Moreover, if a sales and marketing effort fails to target, attract and close new customers it is probably not worth its expense. A new account brings with it the total value over the expected lifetime of the relationship whereas incremental sales to an existing customer will only produce a one-off benefit.

Why are some front-line operations complacent? In a survey of the sales directors of 217 major UK firms the following emerged.

- Only 35 per cent of firms formally screened markets to identify potential customers which offered a high likely return (most relied on advertising to generate leads or gave sales executives the responsibility for finding new customers).

- Responsibility for finding corporate growth is increasingly given to strategy departments, marketing departments and even consultants. Sales directors are often brought into the business development process too late. They are then asked to 'flog' the product rather than having the resources and expertise to find the most profitable prospects within the market and to serve them accordingly.

- The responsibility of customer development is delegated to field sales personnel. Without clear targets, these personnel are likely to focus on the easiest way of achieving sales/margins rather than seeking to maximize the long-term value of the customer base.

- Some organizations have attempted to increase the 'professionalism' of their sales effort. As a result, the base salary has been increased while commissions have been reduced. This could reduce the incentive to find new businesses. Professionalism has brought with it increases in the paperwork and the bureaucracy associated with new customer recruitment has grown. As a sales person commented about his computer firm: 'I lost interest when I had to fill in 8 pieces of paper to open a new account.'

- Sales directors usually have come up through the ranks and focus more of their energy on managing the 'force' rather than questioning where there may be opportunities and what needs to be done to capture them. This creates a form of myopia which results in the organization missing opportunities within the market.

Through maximizing the sales of existing products/services to the customer base, exploiting opportunities to increase the penetration of the customer's pocket while exploring new potential customers the supplier builds income. Of course, by understanding DCP, the supplier will be able to ensure that the additional income is profitable. The attractiveness of each alternative will vary according to the risk and payback associated with the route.

These opportunities might provoke a major rethink of company strategy. If a firm has traditionally thought of itself as being a manufacturer of a specific product, with investment and experience aligned to that product, it is a radical change to question whether it is worthwhile offering a new product/service to existing customers. Similarly, it is a bold decision to target a new group of profitable customers. Such questions can seem 'too big' for front-line management. Instead they can wait for the CEO or a corporate strategist to set the direction for the business.

This is a terrible excuse. The front line should be continually questioning what the easiest route is to increase customer base profitability and present opportunities back to senior management. This entrepreneurializm is a healthy way of finding new profit streams, improving customer service and challenging the supplier to exploit any latent income opportunities.

RESTRUCTURING PRICING/TERMS

The 1990s have witnessed an inflation drought in the Western world. Customers anticipate that costs will be static and price changes are easily visible. Partly as a result of the low inflation pricing appears to have slipped on the management agenda. As a CEO of a plastics company commented:

> In 1974 every board meeting discussed what we should do about prices. In 1994 pricing was not discussed at all.

Yet in the 1990s, the creative management of margins and prices can have a huge impact on profitability. After all, in a firm making a 6 per cent operating margin, a 2 per cent change in gross margins could swing bottom line profits by plus or minus 30 per cent.

The issue has become even more critical as buyers are finding it easier to compare prices. In 1974 a buyer of plastic washers would have had difficulty in finding the lowest market price. He or she was reliant on the quotes that were received from suppliers. Today price information can be easily compared around the world. Smart buyers model supplier costs of production and can move from one customer to another. In this information rich environment the customer is more powerful and supplier margins face continual erosion. Despite these issues, there are a variety of opportunities to refine margin management to help increase/defend margins.

Value pricing

Many firms still employ cost plus pricing, ie they know what a product costs to produce and mark it up by a fixed percentage. This can result in some products being under or over-priced relative to the market opportunity.

The problem was highlighted in the 1980s in the industrial lubricants market. A leading player within this market developed an agent which prolonged the life of machine lubricants by 70 per cent. The agent cost only £0.50 per packet to manufacture so the product management team felt that a reasonable profit would be achieved by marking the product up to £2.00 per packet. The marketing team failed to recognize that the product had enormous value for the customer and that there was no direct competition. Not only did it save the customer lubricant costs, but it also reduced machine downtime and saved the costs of disposing of the lubricant. When these benefits were totalled up, the customer saved more than £200 per packet of the agent (a payback of 100 times).

Despite this enormous customer benefit, sales did not materialize and the product failed. The supplier conducted a 'post mortem' and discovered reasons for the failure were:

▓ distributors had little incentive to sell the product because they made profits by selling the lubricants to the machine shops (if demand for lubricants fell by 70 per cent the distributors would be out of pocket);

▓ there had been insufficient selling/marketing of the product and customers were not made aware of the benefits;

▓ some customers were sceptical whether the product would work if it was so cheap.

Following this review the supplier recognized that the product had been under-sold and under-priced. The team reasoned that there was no direct competition and customers would be happy if they received a 10 times payback. With an increased selling price the supplier could raise marketing and selling support. The product was renamed, relaunched and repriced at £20 per packet. The dedicated selling operation communicated the benefits to the customer and sales took off. By 1995 it had grown to have sales in excess of £100 million while producing exceptional levels of profit.

Although this is an extreme example, it does highlight that conventional ways of calculating selling prices can be inappropriate. Sales, marketing and finance staff must continually review customer needs, check competitor prices and ensure that the price reflects the true value of the product.

Customer specific pricing

The same product can have radically different values to two different customers. Take sulphuric acid. It is used in the manufacture of automobiles and optical products. An auto factory will typically use a thousand times more acid in a year than an optical plant. A typical sales executive might think that the auto plant is the 'must win' customer. Yet a litre of acid adds more value to an optical supplier than a barrel does to the auto factory. This opportunity was recognized by a progressive French sales executive at a chemicals firm who saw the importance of commercial acid to the optical firm and worked with his production department to develop an easy-to-use packaging system and guaranteed a preferential service. This helped secure a price per litre from the optical firm that was 70 times greater than the auto manufacturer. The optical customer was very satisfied with the special service as it accelerated production and reduced the risk of disruption. The finance director of the supplier was even more delighted as the optical customer produced a larger profit than the auto contract.

It is difficult to price the same product at different levels for two customers while preserving a long-term relationship with both. However, by creatively reviewing the options to tailor the service or customize the product routes can be found. The airline industry offers a good example. Quantas was the first airline to introduce a 'business class' which has been subsequently copied by most other carriers. It perceived that the business traveller was less price sensitive than the person on vacation. Through providing an improved environment and better food, business class has been able to achieve a price premium of 300 per cent over the economy seat, despite the fact that passengers travel the same distance and will arrive at the same time.

A much more sophisticated form of differential pricing has been developed at Direct Line Insurance. This business was established in the mid-1980s as an auto insurance company selling direct over the telephone to the customer. By 1995 Direct Line had become the largest motor insurer in the UK. The growth had been fuelled by having direct customer contract rather than using traditional insurance agents. This centralization of information allowed Direct Line to develop an extensive database which profiles the expected profit/risk of recruiting an individual customer driving a specific type of car. In a matter of seconds a multitude of factors and probabilities can be compared and a quote can be prepared. This expertise, combined with the low selling costs, has allowed Direct Line to undercut traditional, less sophisticated operators. In this way Direct Line has been able to achieve exceptional customer service ratings (for example 98 per cent of customers would recommend Direct Line to a friend) while producing a higher than average profit per customer than the industry average. This direct, low-cost, highly tailored pricing system has proved so successful that virtually all the traditional insurers have been forced to adopt similar systems. Direct Line shows that through differentiation and an enhanced understanding of customer needs, a smart supplier can set the right price for an individual customer.

Customer pricing over time

Suppliers are increasingly clever at managing prices over the course of the customer relationship. Consultancy firms might discount to win a new client and then recover profits in 'Phase 2' of a project. Building societies can attract new customers with low start mortgages and then retrieve profits later in the relationship. The computer software market is going even further. Netscape, the Internet access supplier, gives software free to new customers in the expectation that profits will be generated once the customer is familiar with the software. In each of these cases the supplier is attempting to extract the profit once the customer has been locked in. However, there is a danger with such a strategy. As the relationship develops, the customer will become more sophisticated and might attempt to negotiate lower costs. They might demand 'open-book' accounting, take new tenders, or model supplier costs to negotiate the lowest price. These considerations need to be carefully evaluated to construct the ideal, long-term price architecture.

Success-related pricing

A supplier can engineer its price architecture so that it receives a benefit if the product/service delivers real value to the customer. Merchant bankers can charge success-related fees for providing assistance in a corporate acquisition. Some consultants charge clients a proportion of the savings they find rather than a fixed consulting fee. In heavy engineering projects contracts are being agreed whereby the customer pays a bonus if the project is completed early and the supplier pays compensation if it is late. Meanwhile, some outsourcing firms split cost savings with clients while some specialist software firms only charge when the product has achieved the agreed cost savings. In each of these cases the supplier and customer have found it profitable to adopt success-related pricing.

Such schemes are not new. James Watt, the pioneer of the steam engine, had a canny sense for business. Having designed a steam pump which would extract water from mines he appreciated that the pump was far more cost-effective than the alternatives. Rather than selling the pump to the mine owners he gave it to them free on condition that he would receive 50 per cent of the savings against their existing method of water extraction. Initially the mine owners were delighted; however, the working life of the pump was 25 years and they were soon unhappy about the arrangement. They took James Watt and his 'damned engine' to court and then before Parliament, to break the contracts but failed in the attempt. The machines continued to produce the value that had been agreed and James Watt and his backers continued to make profits.

However, success-related pricing, has its downsides. It can delay payment, be difficult to compute and prove a potential liability. Yet it can prove highly profitable and differentiate a supplier from the rest of the crowd.

Offer a guarantee

A less risky form of success-related pricing is to offer the customer a guarantee. This has several benefits: the supplier obtains the cash up front, only a fraction of customers usually exercise a guarantee, and the scheme is relatively easy to administer. The John Lewis partnership has won huge customer support due to its pledge that it is 'never knowingly undersold'. The approach is equally valid in business-to-business markets. As the procurement manager at a leading European airline commented:

> We have excellent procurement models for the buying of everything from fuel to teaspoons. But a guarantee of service is difficult to quantify and can tip the balance. It moves the discussion onto value and away from just price.

Transparent pricing

CPM International operates merchandising and ancillary sales forces on behalf of organizations like Mars confectionery, Seagram and Cellnet. Each CPM client has an 'open-book' profit and loss account which shows each of the cost areas and the net profitability of the contract. Customers can evaluate each line of the P&L to ensure that they are happy with all the costs. Although an open-book system can create problems, it allows the supplier and customer to work together to maximize mutual value.

Review all pricing structures

Pricing structures can evolve to become excessively complicated. Overriders, retrospective discounts, promotion allowances and payment terms can take on a life of their own. Sales people can enjoy having these various loops and hurdles to broaden negotiation options and a complex terms structure allows them to 'milk' unsophisticated customers. The downside is that insistent customers can extract too much discount while the complexity of the scheme is expensive to monitor and control. Two customers with the same turnover and costs-to-serve could end up paying significantly different prices. Such a rift is dangerous. The unsophisticated customer could find out about the premium they are paying and take their business elsewhere. Meanwhile, the aggressive customer will always feel that there are more savings to be negotiated the next time.

In the 1990s a series of companies have shown the benefits of simple pricing structures. For example, Daewoo, the Korean automotive manufacturer, has introduced a 'what you see is what you get' pricing policy, ie the window sticker shows the final price. The customer does not need to negotiate – they know that they are getting the same deal as everybody else. The majority of customers favour the system. It avoids the pressure of negotiation while ensuring that everybody gets the best deal. Customers also prefer talking to Daewoo's non-commissioned advisors rather than haggling with the eager salespeople employed at other dealers. Simple, clear, trusted pricing structures enhance the perceived value of the supplier's brand and encourage customer loyalty rather than giving the benefits to bargain hunters who can turn out to be unprofitable.

Enhance negotiation skills

Most salespeople are taught how to negotiate with a buyer. They are trained to look for the right body language, how to deal with obstacles and how to capture the 'magic moment'. Although such sources can boost the sales person's confidence, it is an inadequate preparation for the new supplier/customer environment. Smart buyers are increasingly conscious about the total costs of acquiring and using a product. They need to know whether the product will achieve the requisite quality standards, how it will be accommodated into the customer's production process/supply chain and whether it will be the easiest to use.

In such circumstances sales people can be out of their depth. Many sales staff do not make the grade and few sales managers recognize the problem. For example, in some recent research from the United States, sales directors were asked to assess the quality of their key account managers.The purchasing managers from customer organizations were also asked to appraise the same account managers. The difference in opinion is striking (see Figure 6.7).

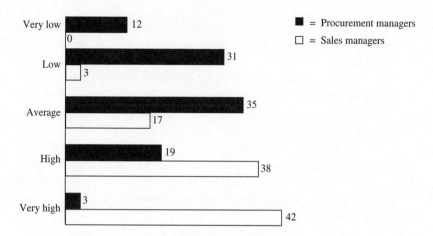

Table 6.7   Rating of account managers by supplier sales
managers and customer purchasing managers
(% of responses)
(Source: Sales and Marketing Management (Aug 1996))

Some organizations sell themselves short because they lack
either the information or people to 'hold their own' against
smart buyers. As a Buyer at Tesco commented:

> Off the record... of the salesmen I see only 20 per cent have
> any decent information and only 10 per cent would be up to
> the standards of our buyers. Some of them have not stepped
> out of the 1950s and don't understand the economics of the
> products they are selling... there is no way that they will negoti-
> ate the best deal.

This gap in ability can result in sales people sacrificing the
margin because it is the only part of the purchase decision
over which they have control. Usually, it is more profitable for
the supplier to enhance the service provided to the customer
rather than capitulating on the margin. Unless the sales person
is familiar with all the routes by which it can reduce the total
costs on behalf of the customer, and improve overall service
the margin will be sacrificed. This requires sales personnel to
be familiar with the wider business issues which are changing
customer needs. Such expertise is critical if sales people are
to hold their own against sophisticated buyers.

Management of pricing and margins is failing to attract the attention it deserves. A creative approach to pricing can allow the supplier to distinguish itself from the competition, increase income, lock-in core profit accounts and nurture the development of the customer base.

7

REDUCE THE COSTS OF INTERFACING WITH CUSTOMERS

Having evaluated the scope for raising income the organization needs to find the most cost-effective means of selling and serving the customer. The supplier must address six questions:

- Which channels?
- What activities?
- Which front-line system?
- Where are activities performed?
- Who/what performs the activity?
- When are the activities performed?

WHICH CHANNELS?

Direct or indirect?

A supplier can either sell direct to the customer or use intermediaries. Over time trade channels might multiply and start to compete against each other. As an example, consider the trade channels employed in the computer software market. The supplier can employ seven main channels, and within each of these there might be hundreds of sub-channels (see Figure 7.1).

Each channel has different associated costs, risks and bene-

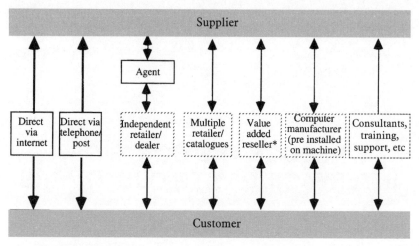

*Uses the software as part of a customer solution.

Figure 7.1 Trade channel options: channels employed by a software manufacturer.

fits. For example, if the software supplier sets up a direct selling route via the telephone it will need to incur substantial costs including:

■ setting up the operation (recruiting and training staff, hiring the premises, etc);

■ obtaining the telephone number of potential customers;

■ handling deliveries to individual customers.

But the direct link has substantial benefits:

■ it allows the supplier to develop an intimate understanding of customer needs;

■ it cuts out any reseller or retailer margins;

■ it minimizes stock within the supply chain;

■ it can be used to increase the support provided by other channels.

For example, Levi's has opened its own stores just as Disney has developed an international retail chain. This direct experience of the retail environment produces a new profit stream, allows a supplier to counter reseller demands for improved margins and provides an opportunity to test innovative ways of retailing merchandise.

Multiple retail channels become dangerous if they go to war and end up fighting between each other for the customer's patronage. The customer can be confused, the overall costs of serving the customer inflate and the commitment of each channel to selling the product can be eroded. To minimize this risk, the supplier should focus the trade channels while considering their strategic importance.

Focus and target trade channels

If a supplier is using multiple channels it should ensure that it balances the requirement for market coverage, channel commitment and cost efficiency.

- *Market coverage.* Just because there are 20 distributors selling a product does not mean that it will reach the customer. The actual availability for the customer should be regularly audited to be confident that no route is being missed.

- *Maximum channel commitment.* If a product is spread too thinly across a broad array of channels it will not achieve the trade backing and sales support it requires. The sales director must trade off the breadth of channel coverage relative to the depth of support.

- *Minimize customer confusion.* Channels should make it easy for the customer to purchase without generating confusion. Too many channels offering different services or prices can bamboozle a customer so they end up buying from a competitor.

Consider the strategic implications of the channel

Through fostering a trade channel, could a supplier be creating problems for the future? A trade channel might over-expose a product, or develop a private label offer which could threaten future income. This was highlighted by RCA, the large US consumer electronics manufacturer. In 1982 it decided to 'go for growth' by supplying the major discount retailers in the US. These low margin/high volume outlets were growing quickly and RCA wanted 'a piece of the action'. Unfortunately, the strategy backfired. These retailers were not interested in selling the high price, top-of-the-range parts of the RCA catalogue. This 'high end' product was where RCA made a high proportion of its profits. Moreover, the discounters demanded aggressive discounts so that they could sell in volume. The volumes did not materialize because in the large stores customers often switched to the even cheaper private label ranges.

RCA not only lost profit by serving these large retailers, but it also upset its old retail 'heartland', the 25,000 high margin/high service specialist retailers that sold its full range. These retailers were being forced to 'price match' against the discounters which operated on a lower cost base and which were receiving a favourable cost price from RCA. Many independents were forced to close, or switched allegiance to other brands, so RCA suffered a sales loss in its core channels. The combination of these factors resulted in a rapid erosion in RCA's profitability. This was finally resolved in 1989 when General Electric repositioned RCA as a lower priced brand for the small/specialist outlets.

A more recent example was seen at Levi's in the UK in the early 1990s. This premium quality denim brand broadened distribution into discount stores. These chains used Levi's as a loss leader which eroded the image and standing of the brand. In the mid-1990s Levi's refined its criteria for supplying an outlet thereby defending the long-term value of the brand.

Channel management has become ever more important with the advent of new selling systems and technology. Computers allow suppliers to manage millions of customers while delivering via specialist distribution firms. As the price of going direct falls, an increasing number of suppliers will be able to take direct control of the customer relationship. Meanwhile, branded suppliers are increasingly suspicious of resellers and retailers who are overly keen to sell their own-brand ranges. A battle is raging between many suppliers and resellers to secure the loyalty of the final customer. This requires a strategic and focused approach to trade management channels.

Traditionally the development of trade channels rested with the sales director. But the advent of new technology, combined with the problems that can arise as a result of sloppy channel management, mean that the issue has risen on the management agenda. The CEO must carefully examine the relative attractiveness of the different routes for getting to the customer and weave this thinking into the overall corporate strategy.

WHAT ACTIVITIES ARE PERFORMED?

Selling is often perceived as being an integrated activity, however it can be de-constructed into its constituent parts. For example, lead generation, re-seller development, negotiation, administration etc are separate functions. Different customers might require varying amounts of these activities or might need special skills/expertise. This trend is encouraging suppliers to segment their selling activity so that each function is performed by the most cost effective resource.

Prioritize the activities/areas of spend

Set up a working party with a sample of customers to determine what they require in terms of service. List the activities and evaluate their relative importance. There are numerous techniques which can test the importance of an activity, but the simplest is to get your managers and customers to rate the important activities from one to five (1 = least important, 5 = most important) and to ask your customers to rate your firm's performance of each of these activities. You can then prioritize those activities which are in most need of improvement. Figure 7.2 shows the results of this analysis for a food manufacturer. At the time the supplier had significant resources deployed delivering and selling to individual outlets. Although this service was highly rated relative to the competition, it transpired that it was of low importance to the customer.

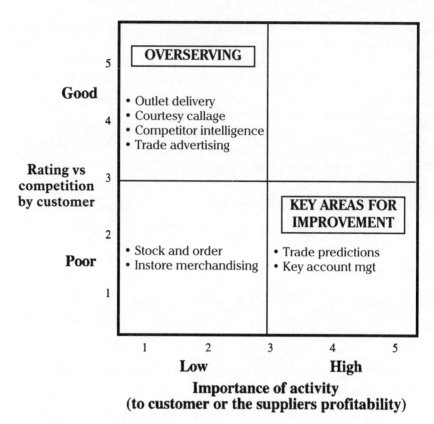

Figure 7.2   Prioritizing most important activities: food manufacturer's selling operation.

Conversely, customers were disappointed by the trade promotions that the supplier operated and it was doing a worse job of managing key accounts relative to the competition. It quickly became apparent that the supplier was 'under-serving' on those factors which were important to the customer while 'over-serving' in less crucial areas. This simple analysis helped explain why the supplier was losing share relative to its major competitor.

However, the supplier must be careful not to take customers' comments at face value. Customers can say one thing and do something totally different. Factors which are deemed of low importance can be crucial in closing the sale. Take, for example, telephone selling. Customers will usually claim that they hate teleselling, yet many will still buy when they are contacted on the phone. Likewise, most customers believe that the personality of a salesperson is unimportant when deciding about a purchase. Yet the closure rate of two salespeople can vary by 100 per cent. It is therefore prudent to test any adjustments to marketing, sales or service and review the impact it has on the bottom line prior to making changes.

Having identified the activities which are important to producing sales, you need to review the effort spent performing the activity. Get the front-line managers to check the time taken per activity and the frequency it is performed per customer per annum. This gives the total effort associated with the job. By plotting the effort against the importance of the activity you can start to identify what needs to be fixed. Figure 7.3 illustrates this exercise for the food manufacturer.

Activities which consume a lot of effort but are of little value should be reviewed and cut back. Meanwhile, all parts of the front line should be focused on the activities which improve customer profit/satisfaction and increase income. Following this analysis, the food manufacturer recognized that it was time to cut back on its van selling operation, prune the sales effort and reduce its trade advertising. Meanwhile, investment was made to enhance trade promotions and beef up key account management. Some activities can be removed altogether either by improving supply chain efficiency or educating the customer. For example, most McDonald's customers have been educated to put their rubbish in the bin so that McDonald's do not require table cleaners. Meanwhile, most orange juice cartons arrive at a shop on a pre-merchandised tray so that they can be put straight onto the retailer shelf. This saves retailers time and cuts out the need for merchandisers to tidy the shelves.

WHICH FRONT-LINE BUSINESS SYSTEM IS APPROPRIATE?

The business system used for deploying front-line resources must be carefully evaluated. Take as an example the maintenance operation which serves a chain of pubs. The equipment which dispensed the drinks was temperamental and was being operated by bar staff who were on low wages. Breakdowns would frequently occur, particularly on busy

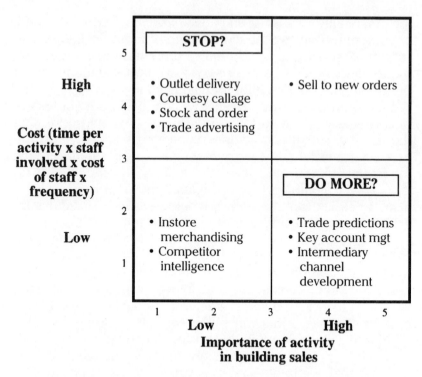

Figure 7.3   Prioritization of resources to have maximum impact: food manufacturer's selling operation.

nights. The service director had the problem that if the system went down on a Friday, he had insufficient staff to get it going again by Saturday night. This could risk the pub losing hundreds of pounds of sales.

Although he perceived the problem as being a lack of staff at key times, it was really because the system was inappropriately structured. Rather than increasing the capacity of the business to handle breakdowns it was better to avoid the problem altogether. Having identified the real issue the director rethought the entire business system. Maintenance engineers were tasked to complete routine, pre-emptive service checks. Through visiting each pub on a fixed cycle, even though the equipment was working properly, engineers could identify a problem before it happened. Moreover, the engineers spent each service call checking that the bar staff were using the equipment properly and that the landlord understood how to make minor repairs. This pre-emptive maintenance reduced the level of breakdowns by 60 per cent and reduced the overall costs of maintenance. In the long term, the brewery recognized that it was cost-effective to buy more reliable equipment to further reduce the need for maintenance.

Just as service departments might be adopting the wrong business system, the sales and marketing departments could be employing an inappropriate model for customer recruitment. They might be spending advertising money to generate customer enquiries and then using the sales operation to close the sale. This conventional recruitment system can be very wasteful. Marketing might build awareness in tens or hundreds of people of whom only one might become a customer (see Figure 7.4).

The conventional 'blitz the market and then sweep up the prospects' approach can prove an expensive way of fishing in a market. Marketing, sales and service departments can spend a lot of time addressing customers who have a slim likelihood of becoming a recruit. Moreover, because the front line is attempting to cover a broad array of potential customers it can fail to obtain a clear understanding of the requirements of the hot prospects. As a result the hit rate can be low.

Database marketing combined with lower cost communications has allowed suppliers to rethink this business system. A supplier can identify and target those customers which are likely to become good prospects. Not only does this business system reduce effort but it can also improve the dialogue with attractive customers (see Figure 7.5).

The supplier needs to question whether it is adopting the right approach to identifying, targeting, winning and serving customers. It is quite likely that the front-line business system was designed when the firm was young, when markets were growing quickly and when prospects were plentiful. In much of the Western world suppliers are now faced with markets which are mature and where new customers are scarce. They cannot afford to waste effort and resources targeting inappropriate customers while failing to properly manage and respond to the most attractive prospects. Across the front line

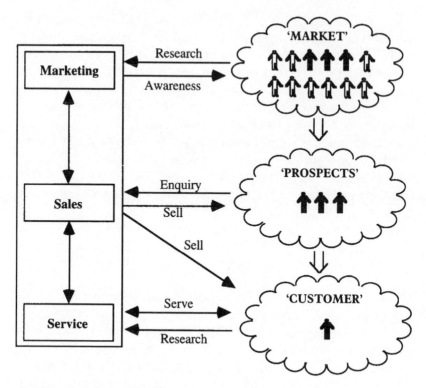

Figure 7.4 Conventional customer recruitment system.

directors must question whether they have the right business system for maximizing long-term profits or whether they are spending time trying to improve what is a flawed approach to interfacing with the customer.

WHERE ARE ACTIVITIES PERFORMED?

All customers do not require or want the same kind of service. Managers at the interface should review whether activities can be segmented and deployed against the appropriate customer types. This marshalling of resources should be determined by the value of the customer or to the extent that a customer is prepared to pay for a different service.

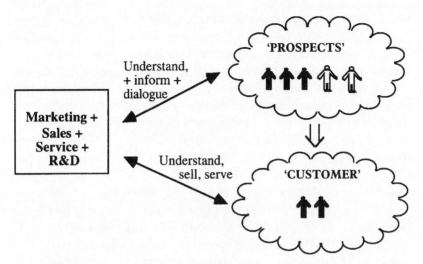

Figure 7.5   Focused customer recruitment system.

Differential service according to the value of the customer

All customers are not created equal and core profit customers can warrant better service. Take as an example Debenhams, the UK department store. A typical customer will spend £60 pa while Debenhams store card holders spend a higher level. Card holding customers who spend more than £500 per annum are particularly important.

Debenhams is committed to improving the service to all customers. Through offering a no-quibble guarantee, friendly staff, good stock availability, reasonable prices, spacious changing rooms, etc Debenhams has achieved a very high level of customer satisfaction relative to the competition. However, store card holders warrant even better service. They receive invites to special preview evenings where wine and food is served. Card holders also receive special mailings, discounts and additional services such as the free alteration of garments. Those customers who spend more than £500 receive even better service. They have their own lounge where free coffee is served, they are known by the store manager, receive special treatment and receive targeted promotions. Meanwhile at Nieman Marcus, the upmarket US department store, customers who spend $75,000 receive first-class air travel and luxurious accommodation at special events.

Offering such elaborate services to all customers would prove unprofitable. However, in each case the incremental investment in the large spending customers has increased profits because annual transactions have been built and retention improved. Debenhams and Nieman Marcus have increased the sales and profitability of the most profitable part of the customer base.

Business-to-business selling can also require differential service. For example, Reuters provides instant service, R&D support and key account managers to major accounts. This exceptionally high level of service could not be justified to small accounts. A useful way of reviewing whether a customer is being under- or over-serviced is to plot the costs of serving the customer against the DCP (see Figure 7.6).

If certain customers are receiving a disproportionate level of service relative to their value, front-line managers should review whether the costs of service can be reduced. Maybe telesales can be substituted for a field representative call or maybe the customer should receive a standard rather than customized service. Equally managers should review whether high value/low cost-to-serve customers are being underserved. This group are of greatest attraction to a potential competitor and might be at the greatest risk.

Differential service according to what the customer will pay

Customers are often prepared to pay for an enhanced service. If you send a letter across London it costs 19 pence for a second class stamp, 25p for a first class stamp, £3.60 for a guaranteed next day delivery or £12.00 for a courier. The same customer might use all these services in the same afternoon because they are prepared to pay a premium price for enhanced service. As the customer is prepared to pay a varying amount for the service, the supplier must ensure that the costs of service are apportioned correctly. A

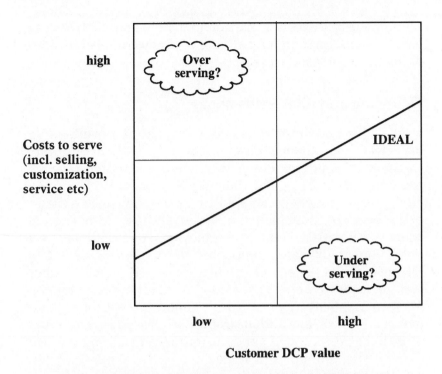

Figure 7.6   Marshalling customer service to DCP.

customer who is seeking the lowest price does not require a Rolls-Royce service. Because customers need varying degrees of service, a supplier can introduce a separate charge and costing structure to reflect this need. For example, Dixons, the electrical goods retailer, offers a series of service packages to its customers. If a customer purchases a computer they can buy a parts and service guarantee or can pay to have an engineer visit the home to install or upgrade the machine. The costs and risks of Dixons offering this service have been separately identified, controlled and passed back to the individual customer.

The proper costing of service is even more important in business-to-business markets. The days of having a large, expensive service operation waiting for a customer to call have passed. Service costs need to be separately identified and allocated back to the individual customer. Without such accountability there is a danger that front-line costs will be higher than required and that core profit customers are subsidizing the troublesome areas.

Financing and after-sales costs

In its eagerness to make a sale a supplier can overlook the bad debt and finance costs associated with a customer. Conducting a proper credit evaluation and confirming the payment structure is not difficult. For example, the major credit cards can check an applicant's worthiness in a matter of seconds by matching the home address with a credit agency database. Through employing state-of-the-art systems, the credit card companies have reduced bad debt. Effective management of credit recovery is equally important. As Figure 7.7 shows, a slow payer can depress net contract profitability by 30 per cent. In essence, poor management of the administration of customers can erode profitability, resulting in good customers subsidizing the bad. Over-serving an unprofitable account at the expense of core profit customers is a dangerous strategy.

	Customer A	Customer B
Contract value	£3000	£3000
Payment	30 days	90 days
Expected contract profitability	£300	£300
Interest charges for delay	-	£75
Admin costs for delay	-	£25
Net contract profitability	£300	£200

Figure 7.7 Managing the cost of credit between customers: printing suppliers.

WHO/WHAT PERFORMS THE ACTIVITIES?

Having identified the activities that will be performed and which customers will receive what service, the supplier must ensure that its resources are deployed effectively. Marketing, sales and service personnel tend to be very expensive. As Figure 7.8 shows, the typical sales person costs £49.4k, of which 57 per cent of the spend is absorbed by indirect charges. Unfortunately, much of their time is spent performing relatively unimportant activities. For example, travel often accounts for 35 per cent of a sales person's time (see Figure 7.9). In order to get the most value from the front line, the manager must creatively marshal the resource by segmenting the activities, removing duplication and using the most cost effective mechanisms.

Remove duplication

Trade structure can become unduly complex with different divisions or trade channels serving the same customer. For example, A S D'Amato, the Chairman of Borden Inc in the US, commented in *Business Week*:

> We had 28 different people dealing with Walmart. It was astounding me.

Meanwhile, the procurement director of a large German publisher produced 32 business cards when asked who he would phone if he had a problem with a certain supplier. He admitted that his life would be a lot easier and the supplier would save money if he only had three contacts. It later transpired that the supplier could save £120,000 per annum by reducing the duplication from the relationship while improving overall customer service.

Not only does duplication produce waste, but it also reduces the credibility of the supplier. Fifteen representatives from the same supplier will receive less attention than one negotiator who represents all 15. Worse still, duplicate representatives from a supplier can compete with each other to win the customer's patronage. This can result in the buyer 'playing off' divisions from the same supplier to improve service and terms.

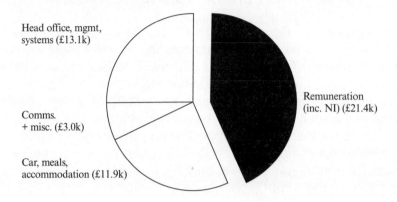

Figure 7.8   The true costs of a sales person.
(Source: Reward Group/SQB Research Centre, Dec 1996)

In order to reduce duplication, while strengthening the overall customer relationship, the supplier should produce a customer decision-making map. This plots the decision makers
resident with the customer and marshals the supplies
people/trade channels who will be responsible for linking with

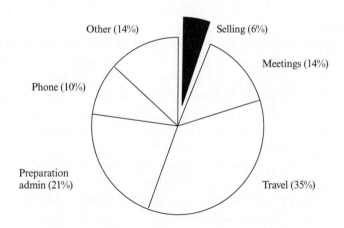

Figure 7.9   Typical spend of a sales person.
(Source: Abberton Associates survey of 74 firms)

the decision maker. A clear account map reduces costs, simplifies matters for the customer and increases supplier clout.

Segment the activities

Increased cost-effectiveness can be achieved by segmenting sales and service functions to ensure that a given activity is performed by the most cost-efficient resource. For example, a leading UK financial services organization used to ask its sales representatives to develop their own leads. However, a sales executive had a total cost of £45,000 (including salary, national insurance, car, benefits and indirect costs). It made little sense having these expensive staff on the telephone when telesales staff could be employed at a much lower cost. Moreover, sales executives grumbled about telephone selling as being a waste of their time while telesales staff were enthusiastic about the responsibility. As a result the telephone sales team achieved a higher conversion rate per call. Consequently the cost of a new lead was reduced from £180 to £45 (see Figure 7.10).

Overall effectiveness increased because field sales executives spent more time working with prospective customers and the telesales unit generated more leads. The combined impact was to increase the number of new customers by 15 per cent on a selling budget that was scaled down by 30 per cent.

Across the front line there are opportunities to segment activities so they are provided by the most appropriately skilled, cost-effective staff and technology. For example, a telephone call is cheaper than a face-to-face visit and an e-mail is cheaper than the telephone (see Figure 7.11).

All these mechanisms need to be evaluated to develop a better service at a lower cost. For example, the cards division of American Express has focused effort where it has maximum impact on customer service while reducing effort. American Express has cut the time required to manage overdue accounts by centralizing essential databases. Prior to the improvements an account analyst needed to make 22 queries when reviewing a problem account. This was time-consuming and expensive; now, thanks to 'Knowledge Highway' (a cen-

	Field sales executive	Telesales staff	Δ
Cost per hour (£)	23	10	-56%
Calls per new lead	14	12	-14%
£ per new lead	**180**	**45**	**-75%**

Figure 7.10 Identifying the most cost-effective resource: cost of setting up a lead for a financial services supplier.
Source: Abberton Associates research.

tralized management information system), the information can be obtained from one data source. Problem accounts can be dealt with more quickly, data accuracy has improved and the cost of processing a query has fallen.

Improved information management has also allowed American Express to change the types of people it employs to manage overdue accounts. Previously, an account manager

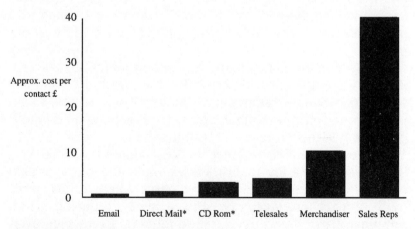

*Note. Depends upon the size of production

Figure 7.11 Costs of contacting customers in the consumer goods market.
Source: Abberton Associates survey of 218 UK selling organizations.

needed to be able to analyse lots of information. This required analytical staff with basic accountancy skills. The system can now undertake much of the numerical work in a fraction of the time. Account managers are now recruited who have strong inter-personal and customer management skills. Furthermore, because the account information is being gathered centrally, it can be analysed to identify common profiles of overdue accounts which allows pre-emptive management of the customer base. American Express has thereby reduced the administration effort while improving overall customer service and satisfaction.

Front-line directors should be continually evaluating whether through segmenting an activity lower cost mechanisms can be employed to improve customer service.

WHEN ARE THE ACTIVITIES PERFORMED?

Right timing is in all things the most important factor.
(Hesiod, Greek poet, 600 BC)

In a world where a new product is lucky if it is famous for 15 minutes, timing is critical. Yet many organizations fail to have the resources when they are most needed because selling and service costs are fixed despite the activity load being peaky. Suppliers attempt to keep the front line busy during the quiet periods, yet the activities tend to have only a marginal benefit. Instead the sales and service directors need to be able to 'turn on and off' the activity when it is really required. They need to be able to provide fire-power when it has the maximum impact.

British and American retailers have been particularly successful at making front line costs variable. In the 1970s most stores worked five and a half days per week with standard hours of 9–5. Today stores are open when the customers want to shop. Moreover, clever staff scheduling systems and the adoption of key timers have ensured that staffing levels match the demand. Queues are shorter, opening hours are 25 per cent longer and Christmas service is better, yet labour costs as a percentage of store turnover have fallen.

Banks and many business-to-business selling organizations have been much slower to change. They are often stuck with a fixed cost front line which is too expensive during quiet periods and has insufficient capacity to handle the peak loads. The resulting slow and patchy roll out of a new product can allow an acute competitor to seize the advantage.

To evaluate the opportunity to make costs variable, the front-line manager should plot staff costs against the level of activity by the relevant time period. For example, Figure 7.12 shows the mix of sales in a chain of pubs relative to the staffing rota. It quickly became apparent that the chain was missing sales at peak times on Fridays and Saturdays while being overstaffed earlier in the week. Through reducing the full-time staff payroll and taking on more 'key timers' at busy periods, the pubs were able to increase weekly sales by around 4 per cent.

In business-to-business selling this analysis is far more complex. Product lead times can stretch over months and a major new product initiative might only take place once every three years. Moreover, the staff have higher skill requirements so it is harder to find 'key timers' when they are needed. Despite these problems Mars confectionery has overcome this problem in Europe by employing auxiliary sales forces and merchandisers

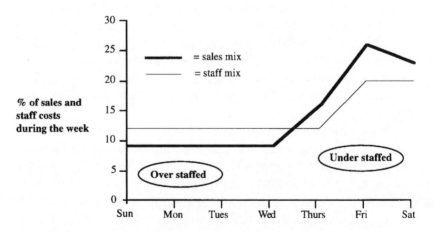

Figure 7.12   Deployment of staff for greatest impact:
sales vs staff mix in a pub.

Source: Mix of sales vs staff rota for a UK pub.

to 'variabilize' activity according to when they will have the most impact. These staff are employed via a third-party specialist supplier. Lotus (part of the global software firm) adopted a similar system. As the sales director commented:

> The beauty of the MSA team (a team of part-time sales personnel managed by a third party) is that it is totally flexible. We can provide incremental reseller support at key times of the year such as during peak buying periods or during the launch phase of a product.

Through the careful use of auxiliary sales forces, teleselling agencies, specialist distributors and third-party support services, the smart front-line manager can provide the fire-power when it is needed without increasing overall costs.

SUMMARY

By fundamentally reviewing what activities are performed, where they are carried out, who performs them and when they are needed, major efficiencies can be realized. Figure 7.14 shows how, by evaluating every aspect of its selling operation, a major financial services organization was able to halve its costs of serving the customer base.

At IBM a similar breakthrough in the cost-effectiveness of the selling operation has been achieved. Having experienced the pressures of increased client sophistication, intense competition and margin erosion in the 1980s, IBM was forced to improve customer service while reducing selling costs. As a result:

- third-party, value-added resellers (VARs) are increasingly being used to service small specialist accounts;

- IBM are employing direct mail and the telephone to service low margin customers;

- the sales organization has been restructured into 14 industry-specific teams to increase the expertise and accountability of the selling effort;

- this has reduced the size of the IBM salesforce from

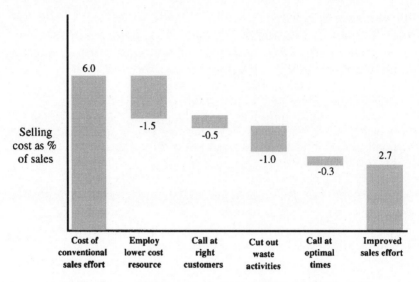

Figure 7.13   Cost savings through improved field
management: financial services supplier.

around 140,000 staff in 1990 to around 70,000 staff in 1994,
producing over $1.5 billion of savings;

IBM has retrained thousands of staff to become consultants rather than sales personnel. This allows clients to pay
separately for value-added services. Moreover, it estab-
lishes IBM as a solution provider rather than being a mere
hardware vendor.

These changes have been fundamental in redirecting and
restructuring the IBM sales effort, and the results appear positive. The satisfaction of IBM customers is improving, sales are
picking up and the cost of sales is falling (see Figure 7.14).

This is a time of immense change at the front line. Suppliers
cannot be stuck with a confused or contradictory trade channel strategy or an inefficient and ineffective front line.
Suppliers need to continually improve the cost efficiency of
the front line to provide exceptional service at a lower cost. A
marketing, sales or service director might be tempted to trim
the size of the existing department or move around the
'deckchairs'. This will not be enough. Every aspect of manag-

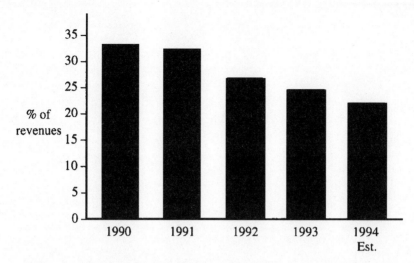

Figure 7.14   Reduction in sales and general and administrative expenses for IBM's sales force as per cent of revenue.
Source: IBM (1994) Business Week, 30 May.

ing the customer base needs to be re-evaluated. The direct or indirect routes employed, the activities undertaken and the technology used must all be rethought. Just as the 1970s and 1980s saw a major shake-out in those employed in factories, in the 1990s and 2000s colossal restructurings are required in marketing, sales and service divisions to improve cost-effectiveness.

8

HARNESS THE TECHNOLOGY

Front-line management can draw upon an unparalleled array of technology including: control systems (computerized customer databases, sales order process systems), communications (electronic data interchange, e-mail, the Internet, mobile phones, video conferencing) and service systems (interactive screens, intelligent telephone systems and automatic diagnostic processes). The expansion of this armoury is a product of the computer and communications revolution. In the past eight years the microchip has become 25 times more powerful and costs much less to produce. As the technological revolution continues the harnessing of customer base systems will be critical to improving the management of customers while reducing costs.

CONTROL SYSTEMS

Marketing, sales and service departments have been slow-comers to the computer revolution. Whereas most company payrolls, accounting systems and production processes are computerized, front-line divisions are often dependent upon pen and paper.

Customer databases

Few companies have even invested in effective customer databases. Instead they rely upon a computerized sales ledger and written customer records. Customer records can be haphazardly stored in a sales executive's briefcase, in a manager's filing cabinet or are hidden amongst the databases used by the finance department. This is probably the most valuable information the supplier holds and yet it is often the least well managed.

The credit card companies are showing the way. Through monitoring and analysing account spend patterns, household socio-graphics, and customer information they are able to construct sophisticated customer databases. Customized mailings are now sent to individual card holders to increase the level of spend while bad debt is controlled. The credit card firms are already miles ahead of most suppliers but even so, companies like Visa are already on the threshold of the next generation of customer base intelligence. Smart cards store far more data about the individual customer and their purchasing behaviour. This will further help to prevent fraud, reduce processing costs and provide new routes for revenue generation.

The value of constructing an appropriate customer base has been demonstrated by a leading UK financial services firm. The company had a long history of selling its products via direct mail and had been very successful in offering a number of different financial services. However, it kept information regarding its million customers on three main databases so it was difficult to tell which customer was using what financial service. This meant that the firm needed to send out 'blanket mailings' which were expensive and achieved a low response rate. It was also difficult to increase the share of the customer's pocket because the supplier's selling operation did not know what service the customer was already using.

Following the integration of all customer information on to a single database the supplier was able to reap immediate benefits:

- Rather than sending out blanket mailings which achieved a response rate of 2 per cent, the firm sent precisely targeted mailings which achieved a 17 per cent response. This increased recruitment while reducing mailing costs.

- All parts of the front line could use the same data to

improve performance. For example, the marketing department identified that a customer who had purchased in the
previous 1.5 years was 10 times more likely to purchase
again than a normal customer. Meanwhile the risk management department identified the profile of customer types
which would produce the greatest payment problems.

To centralize the databases, the supplier had to adopt a new
system which required a significant investment and three
months of installation. Small firms might argue that they cannot
justify the investment. This excuse holds no water. Take an
example – the Amore Pizza and Pasta restaurant in Lompoc,
California. This outlet turns over $1 million pa and has invested
$10,000 in a PC-based customer database. The system moni-
tors the behaviour of the 8500 retail and delivered customers
and assists in finding business opportunities. For example, if a
regular has not been in for a couple of months the system will
send them a special offer to encourage the customer to visit.
Partly as a result of harnessing the value of the customer database, the business has grown threefold in four years. Small
flower shops, hotels and garden centres are also utilizing computers to offer a better level of customer service.

Firms of all sizes need to make the investment in fast, accurate, intelligent customer databases. To prick the conscience
of a complacent CEO, it is worth considering that a small
flower shop near Oxford has a detailed customer base which
has the capacity to send reminder notes to customers regarding their families' anniversaries, birthdays and special occa-
sions. The typical value of the shop's customer is worth only
£40 per annum, yet it has made investment in a decent customer base. It is inexcusable that a major supplier can forget
crucial details about a million pound customer because its
'systems are not up to it'.

Sales order process systems

The computerization of the sales, order and service process is
equally important. A director at the interface should be able to
quickly compare the effectiveness of one individual versus

another. In the UK only 42 per cent of UK sales directors have the systems to easily monitor this performance. The slow adoption of this technology is due to a number of factors:

▦ companies are reluctant to invest to computerize a field person;

▦ the sales manager fears that experienced sales staff will reject the new technology;

▦ there are lots of examples where the computerization of the field force has been over-hyped and under-delivered;

▦ companies do not have a clear understanding of how the technology will pay back.

This last point is critical. Unless there is a clear plan as to how the technology will raise the cost-efficiency and effectiveness of the front line, the benefits will not materialize. Prior to adopting the system, the front line director must detail the benefits that are being sought, the process that will facilitate the improvement and a test of the system prior to roll-out. With this properly thought-out approach the organization can plan for an improvement in cost effectiveness of 20–30 per cent (see Figure 8.1). Otherwise the system will flop.

COMMUNICATIONS

A huge percentage of front-line time is spent communicating. A sales representative might be on the phone to their customer, manager, service department or finance unit. Presentations, quotes, contracts, invoices and payment can all be slow and time-consuming. Yet technology provides short-cuts. For example:

▦ introducing electronic data interchange between a major food manufacturer and a multiple grocer saved the work of eight people;

▦ a video conference link can save days of travel per year;

▦ a car phone can increase the productivity of a sales executive by 10 per cent.

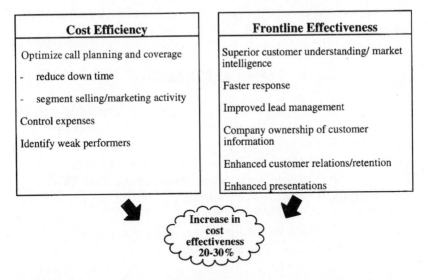

Cost Efficiency	Frontline Effectiveness
Optimize call planning and coverage - reduce down time - segment selling/marketing activity Control expenses Identify weak performers	Superior customer understanding/ market intelligence Faster response Improved lead management Company ownership of customer information Enhanced customer relations/retention Enhanced presentations

Increase in cost effectiveness 20-30%

Figure 8.1   Harnessing sales/order management systems.
Source: Abberton Associates survey of 12 UK sales organizations.

To evaluate whether communication linkages can be enhanced it is worthwhile mapping out all the communications with a typical customer for a working week. How many letters, faxes, invoices, telephone calls and meetings are conducted? How many of these could be shortcircuited or automated? Could an e-mail system reduce the number of telephone calls? Could an automatic payment system be introduced to save time in the finance department?

As a role model it is worth considering the National Lottery in the UK. A customer can purchase a ticket from an outlet only one hour before the draw. The customer's numbers will be processed and logged and they will receive a receipt in less than two seconds. Cash is automatically transferred from the retailer bank account to the National Lottery. The system can handle more than £100 million per week from over 30 million customers via 30,000 outlets with virtually no problems.

Communication systems are allowing a faster and more accurate dialogue between supplier and customer. Firms need to explore all the options in order to improve the linkages between the various parts of the front line and with the customer.

SERVICE SYSTEMS

A new range of technology is becoming available which improves service support. For example, the Nationwide building society is testing eight branches which use multimedia touch-screen systems to provide instant customer service. Daewoo, the Korean auto firm, uses interactive kiosks to demonstrate the features of their cars rather than employing a pushy salesperson with a brochure. The system contains extensive user-friendly information about the car and allows customers to review different colour options, features, etc. Customer response to the technology is favourable. It allows customers to receive information at their own pace and the system costs only 5 per cent of the cost of a sales representative. Meanwhile a car driver can fill the tank with gasoline and pay by swiping a credit card rather than having to join a queue at the till, a hotel guest can check out without waiting at reception and an airline passenger can confirm details of a flight by speaking to a clever telephone response system. A customer can buy a can of Coke from a cool vending machine rather than going into a shop. At Safeway customers can self-scan their merchandise rather than putting it through the checkout and most customers are happy using a cashpoint rather than a bank.

All these examples illustrate how technology is being adopted to improve customer service while saving the supplier money. Technology can also be used to simplify the activities carried out by service staff. The RAC Recovery breakdown service now carry CD-Roms which detail the workings in every UK automobile. Rather than carrying bulky parts manuals the engineer can quickly use the CD-Rom technology to help diagnose and rectify problems. Likewise, if you have a problem with your PC, a service engineer from Digital MCS can, via a modem, see what is on your screen and discuss the problem on the telephone even though the engineer is based hundreds of miles away.

Customers are increasingly comfortable with this new technology and prefer receiving an immediate, accurate response, rather than waiting for the slow response from a traditional service unit.

E-COMMERCE

The popularization of the Internet and interactive TV-shopping draws attention to the new technology which is allowing direct relationships between supplier and customer. On a PC with connections to the Internet, a customer can visit 'Barclay Square', shop at the virtual Sainsbury's and book a holiday without leaving home.

Although the Internet is much discussed as a home shopping medium, it is already revolutionizing the business-to-business market place. Price Waterhouse estimates that by 2002 over $400bn of trade will be conducted on the web, of which over $300bn will be business-to-business. Every aspect of the interface is being re-thought. Selling, ordering, customisation and payment can all be handled via e-commerce. As an example, consider Chrysler. It now connects with small dealers via the web. This has allowed transactions which used to take three weeks to be completed in 24 hours, involving millions of paper based purchase orders and invoices. The internet will also have a profound impact on the selling of complex products and services which are digitizable and have high interface costs. A good example is the selling of financial services. An investor who uses a stockbroker currently receives lots of waste paper – brochures detailing stocks which are of no interest, paperwork and various statements. The existing services can be expensive, slow and inefficient. Computer services, on the other hand, allow a customer to find the information of interest to them. Information can be customized so that they get the data they require rather than having to sift through unnecessary papers. For example, Merrill Lynch are undertaking exciting developments where it will electronically notify customers of news which is relevant to them. Merrill Lynch, a customer owning General Motors' Stock, will be automatically notified of GM's news and performance. Likewise, Fedex has introduced a tracking service on the Internet which allows customers to book a delivery, or to see where a parcel is. This saves the customer time and also means that Fedex save a significant cost in telephone staff. This internet service is 80 per cent cheaper than the conventional order system but provides customers with a faster and better service.

Other industries which have expensive selling systems will be able to harness the technology to provide better service at a lower cost. Estate agencies, auto dealers, pharmaceutical sales, information services, travel and business-to-business selling will face enormous change as a result of the new communications systems.

Of course, there will be short-term problems. The slowness of some communications, and financial security problems, will depress adoption. Moreover, some customers are not ready for the new technology. For example, when the Oslo stock exchange attempted to provide up-to-date stock prices on the Internet, it had to pull the service because only three companies subscribed. Despite these teething problems, the direct low-cost technology will open the door to a new generation of high-tech competition. This threat means that all companies, particularly those with a complex product and a high cost of serving the customer, need to be exploring the new technology.

SUMMARY

New technology has the potential to transform every customer/supplier relationship. A front-line director in the 1990s should be spending at least two weeks a year contemplating how new technology might improve the cost-effectiveness and the service provided by the front line. There is a temptation to delegate this responsibility to the computer department or an external vendor. But this can miss the opportunity. Whereas a marketing, sales or service director can appreciate how an application will strengthen the customer relationship, a computer person tends to put the technology before the relationship. Moreover, the front-line director must take responsibility for ensuring that control, communication and service systems are interlinked. A fully integrated front-line system reduces effort and improves accountability, thereby providing a better level of customer service at a lower cost.

9

FIX UNPROFITABLE ACCOUNTS

If the supplier has explored all the routes to increase income while improving the efficiency of the front line, the proportion of unprofitable customers should be small. Yet there might remain a rump of unprofitable customers. How can the supplier make these customers profitable or should it terminate the relationship?

The customer base should be ranked by DCP so that the front-line managers can review the profile of the bottom 20 per cent of customers. What is depressing their profitability? Are they generating insufficient sales or producing exceptionally low gross margins? Or are they too expensive to serve?

Having recognized the reason for the lack of profits the supplier can determine whether it is worth investing the effort to turn the customer around. Otherwise, it might be appropriate to serve the customer via a friendly third party. If these routes fail the supplier should drop the customer.

TURNING A CUSTOMER AROUND TO PROFIT

Possibly the customer is too small. Could it be encouraged to order more by introducing a minimum order level or adjusting the pricing structure to stimulate additional sales? Could the costs of serving the customer be reduced by using the telephone rather than having sales representatives visit the outlet? Can small customers be banded together so that selling and administration costs are reduced? Or can the customers be charged for the services they use? Each of the routes should be considered and possibly tested in a workshop with small unprofitable customers.

For example, First Chicago bank in the US identified that small customers which used branch teller services produced little profit. As a result, it has started charging customers which use teller services. The results have been positive. It appears that less than one per cent of these customers were lost as a result of the charges. Some switched to automatic services whilst others were happy to pay for what they were using. Overall income from these customers has increased and First Chicago has been able to reduce its branch staff by 30 per cent.

GIVE/SELL THE CUSTOMER TO A THIRD PARTY

Although a supplier might not be able to make a profit from a customer, it is quite likely that another channel could profitably service the customer. For example, in 1994 one of the UK's cigarette manufacturers recognized that the costs of selling and delivering to small independent outlets were so high that the outlets produced virtually no profit. However, a major wholesaler of convenience products was already serving most of the outlets. By scaling back its direct selling operation while carefully passing the retailers on to the wholesaler's delivery system, the manufacturer was able to restore profits and obtain two benefits: it saved the costs of delivery to the outlets, and because it placed increased volumes via the wholesale channel it commanded superior trade support. Equally, it could be worth attempting to 'sell' the unprofitable parts of the customer base to an organization which could make them profitable. For example, when this analysis was undertaken by a delivery business it transpired that customers which were too far away from the distribution centre were not profitable. By selling these areas to independent transport companies, the supplier was able to generate capital for investment in the core service. This served to strengthen the profit stream from the core customers, while not upsetting customers in provincial areas.

In business-to-business selling, specialist distributors or value-added resellers can profitably reach the customers which do not warrant direct service. It is also sensible to deal with groups of unprofitable customers at the same time. By moving a block of business, the supplier is likely to receive more support than if small customers drip through individually to other channels. Moreover, by dealing with these customers as a block it is easier to give them the support they require to facilitate a smooth transition.

DROPPING A CUSTOMER

If the customer is not going to make a profit and cannot be transferred to another channel, the supplier must evaluate whether to terminate the relationship. After all, it is usually better to invest resources in the parts of the customer base which have profit potential rather than continuing to over-serve unprofitable accounts.

If a customer relationship is to be terminated, it should be handled very carefully. An unhappy customer is likely to express dissatisfaction to other potential customers or might be slow in paying outstanding bills. The relationship should be terminated only as a last resort and should be handled consistently and professionally. It might be worth explaining to the customer why it is unprofitable, outlining the options to profit (ie increase sales or take the service from another channel) and agree a path ahead.

Having gone to the expense and trouble of recruiting and developing a customer, it is difficult to contemplate terminating the relationship. However, if the customer is bleeding the supplier's profits and shows no likelihood of producing a profit (which should be reflected in the DCP analysis), the supplier must creatively explore the options to deal with the relationship. This will free up effort to concentrate on the profit opportunities that reside elsewhere in the customer base.

10

MANAGE THE CUSTOMER LIFE STAGES

LIFE STAGE MANAGEMENT

A customer relationship typically involves three stages: recruitment, development and decline. Managing each stage in the customer's life can have a major impact on the bottom line. As an example, let us consider the profit made by an average new recruit for the provider of specialist financial services. Its customers are the treasury departments within large 'blue chip' corporations. A typical customer relationship would be six years and during that time the supplier would make around ₤49,000 profit (see Figure 10.1).

There was a significant deviation in the profile of different customers at the same life stage with some producing a ₤15,000 loss and others producing ₤300,000 of profit. Moreover, some went from recruitment to decline in a matter of months while other relationships stretched over 20 years. Despite this deviation it was appropriate to review individually each stage in the relationship to examine whether profit opportunities were being missed.

ENHANCE RECRUITMENT

Through profiling the make-up of an attractive recruit suppliers can save effort. It might be difficult to spot attractive types of customer. They do not wear a badge which says 'I will spend a lot of money, pay a good margin, will be cheap to serve and will not produce a bad debt.' However, common profiles of

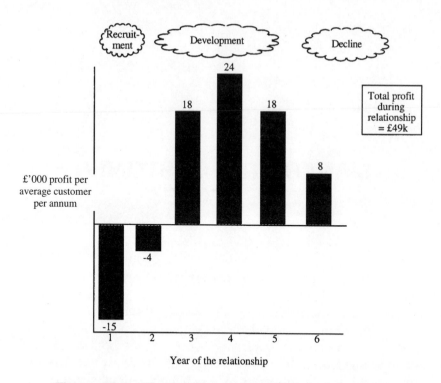

Figure 10.1 Typical life stage profile of a customer.
Source: UK specialist financial service provider.

good customers can be found in terms of market profile (age, sex, etc), customer need (interested in certain features), service requirement (eg will order over the telephone) and credit profile. Through checking these profiles a 'target customer' might become apparent. Even if it is difficult to identify a good prospective recruit, it is usually relatively easy to spot bad practice. For example, the bad debt profile might differ significantly between two sales areas because one representative is 'over-selling' to unattractive recruits.

In order to refine recruitment the supplier should measure the direct and indirect costs of recruiting a new customer (ie the costs of advertising, enquiry handling, sales support and customer service) and then get the front-line managers together to see if it could have been achieved at a cheaper rate. It is also useful to speak to the new recruit to see what could have been done to win their business at reduced expense.

In the case of a financial services supplier, it recognized that its cost of bringing in a new recruit was too high. Approximately £18,000 was being spent per recruit when the advertising costs and front-line time was properly allocated. A new marketing director was appointed who stopped advertising in the trade press and opted for a focused recruitment strategy. He organized specialist forums which brought together the ideal prospective customers and used teleselling to reach prime prospects. He even introduced a 'client get a client bonus' where a customer was rewarded for finding a new prospect. At the same time the sales order process was tightened up so that prospects did not 'slip through the net'. By overhauling and rethinking every aspect of customer targeting and recruitment the supplier was able to reduce the typical costs of account acquisition from £18,000 to £7000 while increasing the number of new recruits.

REFINE ACCOUNT DEVELOPMENT

After three years a typical customer would produce around £24,000 of profit. This was higher than the level achieved by competitors but front-line managers felt that there was more to go for. They saw that although the supplier had a large share of the customer's pocket, there were new revenue opportunities. For example, the sales director ensured that he had representation in all the divisions of a customer by setting up a discount structure which rewarded incremental sales. The supplier also set up a joint venture with a non-competing, specialist information supplier. The two firms developed a management information service which was sold to the core customer base. This generated a highly profitable income stream. Moreover, the supplier found that by refining the services provided, it saved customers money and was able to increase charges. The combined impact of these developments increased the typical profits made in year four of the relationship from around £24,000 to around £35,000.

SLOW THE DECLINE

Partly because the financial services supplier was investing more effort in developing the customer relationship, account retention increased. Moreover, the supplier kept a much closer eye on how a customer was performing and looked for signals to suggest that the relationship was starting to deteriorate. By offering special services at this time and by developing 'lock-in' incentives, a significant proportion of the customers kept their business with the firm. It is too early to estimate the precise impact on the average longevity of a customer relationship. However, it appears to have been extended by over two years.

When considered individually the changes to customer recruitment, account development and management of declining customers do not appear too radical. Yet the impact on the bottom line was profound. The combined benefits meant that the average profit per customer increased approximately threefold (see Figure 10.2).

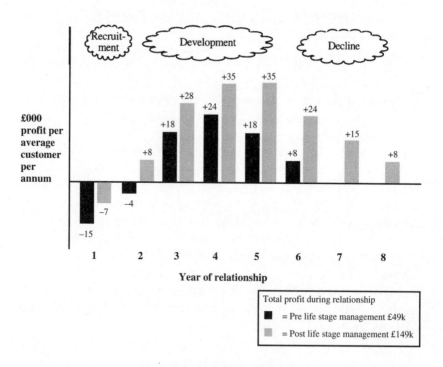

Figure 10.2 Impact on the life stage profile of improving life stage management.

Source: UK specialist financial service provider.

The initiative also realigned the way front-line resources were deployed. Previously, there had been an enormous investment in marketing and selling to win new accounts. Through employing the focused and controlled approach to account development, the costs of recruitment were slashed even though the number of new customers increased. To maximize the income from existing customers and to extend account longevity the supplier deployed more resources later in the relationship (see Figure 10.3).

The impact was quite dramatic. Effort deployed in recruiting new customers was cut by 45 per cent while effort spent developing customers and prolonging their longevity increased by 40 per cent. The advertising agency was unhappy about the shift in resources as the advertising budget was cut and expenditure was shifted into enhanced customer service and improved account management. However, the CEO and shareholders were delighted by the increase in customer profitability.

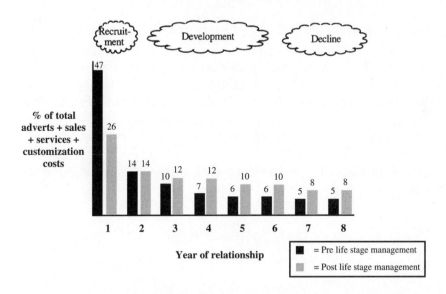

Figure 10.3 Redeployment of front-line resources over the life span of the customer: allocation of total interface costs (%) (including advertising, sales, service, product customization and indirect business relationships).

SUMMARY

In the slow growth markets in the Western world the philosophy of investing in existing customers and reducing recruitment expenditure is persuasive. Advertisers can find that new recruitment activities attract a promiscuous sort of customer who take the special offer but desert when a better promotion comes along. Such behaviour is seen in the newspaper market. While a title is advertising on television or is running a large-scale promotion the readership will pick up by about 5 per cent but as soon as the campaign stops the circulation will usually drop back to the loyal readership level. The true profitability of attracting such promiscuous readers is dubious and a better payback appears to be generated by those titles which focus on developing their core readership. Meanwhile, the Tesco Club Card has shown that a better payback can be achieved by investing in customer loyalty rather than increasing advertising expenditure. This shift in emphasis is sensible in a mature market where more profit can be made by developing an existing customer rather than courting the elusive new customer.

The supplier must review every stage in the customer lifecycle. Through improving the management of recruitment, development and decline, profits can be boosted while service is increased. This review might also question at what stage in the relationship investment should be made. To date many suppliers have been too focused on recruiting new customers while 'milking' the loyal parts of the customer base. In slow growth, mature markets, such an approach can be dangerous.

11

MAKE IT HAPPEN

Changing the way the customer base is managed is tricky and potentially risky. Management need to proceed carefully and use a lot of common sense.

REVIEW THE DCP FOR A SAMPLE OF CUSTOMERS

Ask a financial analyst and a middle-ranking sales or marketing executive to project the DCP for a sample of around 16 customers. This crude analysis should be complete in a couple of weeks. You can then review the customer profile of the sample:

- Is there a significant deviation in the income achieved from different sorts of customers? Is this caused by sales or percentage margins or the costs of interfacing?

- What are the costs-to-interface with the customer? Do they deviate significantly? Why is there deviation?

- How much of your profit comes from the core customers?

- How long will the customer relationship be? Why is it not longer?

- How much effort goes into recruiting a new customer relative to keeping an existing customer?

INTERVIEW A FEW CUSTOMERS

See what is important to them and how your firm scores relative to the competition.

▪ Is your firm scoring well on the factors that really matter?

▪ What are the perceived strengths of the competition?

▪ Do you understand their future needs?

HOLD A WORKSHOP WITH THE FRONT-LINE DIRECTORS

Sales, marketing and service directors should get together in a workshop to evaluate what profits/opportunities reside within the sample of customers:

▪ *Is everything being done to lock in core customers?*

   – Are you surpassing customer expectations?

   – Can the relationship with the customer be elevated?

   – Are the bonds with the customer strong enough?

   – Are you prepared for customer needs?

   – What actions will you take if the customer declines?

   – Should you reward loyalty?

   – Will the above make it more difficult for a competitor to poach your core profit customers?

▪ *Can additional income be extracted from the customer base?*

   – Are existing sales to existing customers fully potentialized?

   – Are there new services which could be provided to existing customers?

   – Do competitors have a more attractive set of customers? Why is this? Can those customers be poached?

- Are there new customer channels which you are missing?

- Should prices or trade terms be realigned?

- Is it worth introducing guarantees, transparent pricing or value pricing?

- Can negotiation strength be increased?

- Does the quality of account management need upgrading?

Can the costs of interfacing with the customer be reduced?

- Should you be selling direct or indirect?

- Can the co-ordination of trade channels be improved to increase income and reduce costs?

- What interface business system should be adopted?

- Is there duplication of effort between sales, marketing and service?

- What activities/spend is required?

- Who is the most cost-effective resource to perform the task?

- Which customer receives what service?

- When should the activities be performed?

Are you harnessing the technology?

- Is the customer database in good shape?

- Can more cost-effective communication systems be employed?

- Are management control systems tight?

- Is it appropriate to introduce customer-friendly service technology?

- How can technology help provide a better quality service at a lower cost than the current system?

■ *What can be done to fix unprofitable accounts?*

- Can the unprofitable customers be turned around?

- Can they be given or sold to a third party?

- Should they be dropped?

■ *Can the life stage management of the customer base be tightened?*

- Can the targeting of prospects and the recruitment process be refined?

- Is there an opportunity to generate more income from an established account?

- Can the attrition of the customer base be reduced to improve account longevity?

- Should more money be spent developing existing customers rather than attracting new ones?

The workshop might take a couple of days. Hopefully lots of ideas, opportunities and issues will arise. It is then useful for the directors to prioritize each opportunity. Guestimate the size of the profit that could be produced and score it out of 5

Area	Opportunity	Size of profit (1-5)	Amount of effort/cost to achieve (3-1)	Overall attractiveness (8 = high priority, 2 = low priority)
Reduce interface costs	Sell direct rather than via intermediaries	4	1	5
	Introduce mobile phones for sales executives	1	3	4
	Introduce differential service by customer type	5	2	7

Figure 11.1 Example of prioritizing front-line opportunities.

(1 = small, 5 = very big). Then estimate the difficulty and cost associated with making a change and score it out of 3 (1 = substantial effort/cost, 3 = easy/cheap to achieve). This should allow sales, service and marketing to 'ball park' the relative attractiveness of the different opportunities. Figure 11.1 illustrates this approach. Overall, the management team should anticipate discussing and prioritizing over one hundred opportunities and options.

These opportunities should then be quantified for each of the sample customers.

By forcing the management team to quantify each route, the scale of the overall opportunity can be appreciated. The summary of this analysis is shown in Figure 11.2. It shows the net customer profitability from a professional services firm. The management team identified significant scope to increase sales to three customers. Margin opportunities were identified for a

Customer	Current contribution £000	Increase sales £000s contribution *	Improve margin £000s contribution **	Reduce costs £000s contribution ***	Target contribution £000s
1	486	198	202	45	932
2	493	713	86		1291
3	527	122	0	18	667
4	408	87	0		495
5	19	134	21	18	192
6	64	30	0		94
7	−6	15	0	14	22
8	22	48	0		70
9	−13	59	0	12	59
10	−13	0	0	14	1
11	−22	65	0	14	58
12	−53	18	0	12	−23
13	−25	55	0	5	35
14	−106	315	1	12	222
15	−18	381	0	6	369
16	−80	12	0	6	−62
Total	1683	2253	309	176	4421

*   Includes six routes to drive sales
**   Includes three routes to improve margins
*** Includes three actions to reduce costs

Figure 11.2 Summary of increasing net customer profitability (professional service firms)

further three customers and interface costs could be reduced by re-structuring the account teams. By driving sales in a focused way, profits could be increased by £2.3m. While margin improvement offered £0.3m and interface costs could be cut by £0.2m. The exercise showed that the real opportunity lay in focusing the selling effort and refining account development.

Despite these improvements, two customers were still unprofitable. One of these was successfully re-priced and the other was terminated. The management team also explored the routes to improve account development, which further increased the DCP. When the sample was scaled up for the entire company it was perceived that profits could be raised by over £15m.

This process is quick and dirty. Some opportunities will arise that can be immediately exploited; however, the workshop is not attempting to resolve all the problems in one day. Rather, it is assisting front-line directors in deciding whether they should focus effort on improving the management of the customer base. If the answer is yes a project team should be assembled to help construct a customer base strategy.

CONSTRUCT A CUSTOMER BASE STRATEGY

Two representatives from finance, marketing, sales and service should make up the core team. These will need to draw on the expertise of other people within their departments. The team should work directly with the front-line directors. The project team should be of the highest quality. After all, any proposals which change the way a supplier interfaces with its customers can have a profound impact on the bottom line. It should be tasked with producing a customer base strategy which details the opportunities, actions required and investment needed over a three-year period. In order to complete this study the team will need to consider the following:

▨ *Measure what matters.* The project team should model the DCP of customers/trade channels. It should also conduct research regarding customer satisfaction, the likelihood of repurchasing, the importance of the activities that are provided for customers and how the supplier is rated relative to the competition. It should also attempt to estimate the profitability of customers which source from the competition. This basic intelligence is crucial to ensure that the customer base strategy is founded on real profit opportunities and the views of real customers.

Formally review the routes to profit. The front-line directors and the team should explore the routes to unlock the value of the customer base, ie

- to lock in and develop core profit accounts;

- to increase income;

- to reduce the costs of interfacing with customers;

- to check the technology options;

- to fix unprofitable accounts;

- to refine customer lifecycle management.

To flesh out the benefits and risks associated with each opportunity, *ad hoc* analysis will be required. Much of this has been described in earlier sections of this book. However, the team should not get bogged down in the analysis. They must continually check that the route which is being explored will have a material impact on long-term profits. It might also be useful to call upon the services of some of the IT and communications firms. Companies like IBM and Unisys have a fantastic understanding of how technology can be harnessed to improve the efficiency and effectiveness of the front line.

In addition to reviewing each of the profit opportunities, the working party should consider three general issues which affect all frontline divisions: what culture, coordination and control mechanisms are required to deliver excellent service to customers while maximizing customer base profitability?

Culture

The culture of an organization can have a major bearing on its ability to exploit opportunities at the customer base. Are

front-line staff committed to the customers they intercon-
nect with? Are they proactive in finding new income opportunities within the customer base? Is the organization
striving to support the front line in developing customers? Is
autonomy delegated to the optimal position within the organization? If the answer to all these questions is no, the supplier has a lot of work to do.

Despite the billions that have been spent indoctrinating
organizations that the 'customer is king', many staff have
proved deaf to the message. One reason for this failure is
because customer service has often been chanted as a
mantra rather than being tied back to the profit of the company and ultimately to the pocket of the employee. By increasing the proportion of remuneration which is aligned to
customer base profits, it is easier to focus all staff on improving customer service. Remuneration is one means to develop
a more customer-focused culture but this will need to be
accompanied by training and effective communications. This
commitment was best illustrated at the launch of the Infiniti.
Every employee in the dealerships was sent on a six-day training course to improve product familiarity and customer empa-
thy. Secretaries, mechanics, managing directors, everyone
was involved. After all, a secretary can often speak to more
customers in a day than a sales person.

Even if the organization is customer-focused many of its attitudes might be inappropriate for the modern trading environment. For example, if the supplier is attempting to forge
partnerships with core customers it will need to change the
mentality of the front line. A gung-ho salesman who is
bonused on sales can be a liability if the supplier is forging a
long-term, strategic relationship. Similarly, the loner mind-set
needs to be redirected if the front line are to function as a
team.

The customer base working party will need to question
whether the culture, attitudes and motivations of the marketing, sales, service and R&D departments are appropriate to
realizing the value of the customer base. By reconsidering staff
recruitment, remuneration and training systems the organization can help ensure that the customer base strategy will be
made to work in the field.

Coordination

If an organization lacks a customer-focused culture, the problem can often stem from poor coordination between front-line divisions. This can degenerate to the point where marketing staff will not even speak to sales staff other than at the conference for a new product launch. Likewise, some R&D staff treat sales and service staff as if they were lepers, locking them out of new product development centres and only canvassing their opinion late in the product development process. This problem is exacerbated if the front-line divisions have non-complementary targets. This was noted by the managing director of the UK subsidiary of a major computer manufacturer:

> Product management were incentivised on the performance of the new generation of products, sales were bonused on selling off the stocks of the old generation and customer service was a profit centre which wanted to repair the old equipment that was already with the customer . . . we had the ridiculous situation where our own departments were competing with each other.

Another example of this disfunctionality was to be found at a major chain of department stores. Department managers were targeted on the profits their departments achieved while store managers were given sales targets. In order to achieve the sales target, store managers often reduced the space provided to high margin departments and gave additional space to low margin departments which produced high sales densities but little profit.

Such problems are surprisingly common. Few firms had common aligned goals for their product management, sales and service divisions. If customer base profits are to be unlocked, it requires all front-line and support divisions to be coordinated so they play as a team. Through reviewing DCP and drawing up a customer base strategy, all divisions have a common understanding as to the best route/routes to profit.

Control

Having identified the routes to profit the project should produce a detailed plan of action which highlights the opportunities to be pursued, the changes required, the costs to be invested and the timescale of the adoption. Ideally this plan should forecast the DCP profitability over the next three years and have a realistic, achievable critical path.

With the strategy in place the team should also ensure that measures are set up to monitor ongoing DCP and customer satisfaction. This will allow management to conduct frequent health checks to monitor the state of progress.

It is useful to remember that any measurement systems should be fed back in an easy-to-understand form for managers and staff. The measurements should be broken down to individual activities over which staff members have some control. For example, if the supplier is planning to increase customer base longevity, each regional sales manager should be provided with information regarding the average length of a customer relationship when compared with the company norm. This should then be decomposed into the reasons for customers terminating the relationship while highlighting exceptionally weak or strong performance.

With the right targets and measurement tools it becomes easier to motivate front-line staff. Motivation of the front line is critical. Those working with customers need to be fired up with energy and enthusiasm. These qualities are difficult to nurture and sustain, yet if staff are confident that they are working together to exploit opportunities the motivation will usually improve.

SUMMARY

The customer base strategy will not be perfect. It will date very quickly as new technology becomes available, the competitive environment evolves and customer needs change. This means that the supplier must continually review the actual profit produced by customers and the effectiveness and efficiency of the system. The overall profitability of the customer base must be continually reviewed, challenged and upgraded. Through constantly reviewing its management of the customer base, the supplier will minimize the risk of being outmanoeuvred by a competitor or being stuck with unnecessary costs.

12

PREPARING FOR THE NEW ERA

A major strategic shift is occurring in the way that customers and suppliers interrelate. To put things in perspective, consider how the marketplace has evolved during the past 300 years. Prior to the Industrial Revolution most producers had a close working relationship with their customers. A blacksmith would know everybody in the village and his production would be tailored to meet their needs. Fitting a horseshoe for the squire, fixing a plough for a farmer and forging a piece of wrought ironwork for the church could all be in a day's work. The customers were diverse but the blacksmith was versatile in satisfying their demands. He could match his production skills to the needs of the customer. This allowed him to achieve a relatively high share of his customers' pockets.

With the coming of industrialization the distance between manufacturer and customer extended. Manufacturers focused on producing a narrow range of products while achieving economies of scale. They were set up with product managers defining market opportunities, factories producing 'mass' quantities, and the sales director was told to sell the stock. Customers had little direct contact with the supplier as they were usually served by the suppliers' agents, dealers, resellers and retailers.

By the 1970s, mass markets in developed countries tended to fragment. This market fragmentation required suppliers to be smarter at spotting the different needs/wants of market sectors. Acute CEOs set about differentiating the product and service. They drove manufacturing processes to be more flexible so that a greater number of products/services could be produced at a reasonably low cost. This meant that all supplier departments had to deal with the complexity associated with different product/service requirements. In some cases suppliers preserved economies of scale through international expansion.

While manufacturers in mature markets saw the fragmentation of customer requirements, their brethren in retail and reseller trades often witnessed the reverse trend. These channels had a close proximity to the final customer and evolved to meet customer needs. This proximity allowed smart, sophisticated multiple retailers to flourish in the latter half of the twentieth century. They could tell what products, services and prices the customer wanted and had the capacity to respond accordingly. Some retailers were then able to broaden their appeal to extract a larger share of the customer's pocket. For example, the discount outlets in the US, hypermarkets in France and multiple grocers in the UK extended their product ranges to include clothing, homewares, petrol, fast-food, flowers, etc. This has allowed major retailers to widen the spread of their customer proposition at a time when many manufacturers have been stuck with market fragmentation.

During the past few hundred years there has been an enormous change in the structure of markets. In the future the pace of change will accelerate. Communication and distribution costs will fall, production processes will become more flexible, computer power will assist in the management of the complexity and customers will become more diverse in their needs and wants. These factors have allowed suppliers to reinvent the way they link with individual customers. For example, in the US Levi's is, in some stores, tailoring jeans to meet the precise needs of the customer. Your exact size and fit will be shipped to your home 24 hours after you have been fitted in the store. Meanwhile, Hallmark Inc., the greetings card firm, has developed a system whereby the customer can select the message they want to put in a card which is then printed in the store. In London, Norton and Townsend, the visiting tailor service, will produce a custom-made suit with only a 20 per cent price premium over buying 'off the peg'. In business-to-business markets the changes are even more profound. Software suppliers can tailor the product to the precise requirements of the customer/user. Meanwhile, plastics moulding firms can manufacture 'one-off' components at low cost by working in partnership with the customers

The combined impact of computer-aided design, low-cost direct communication systems (eg the Internet, video conferencing and the telephone), effective customer base management systems and agile manufacturing processes mean that suppliers have the opportunity to function more like the old village blacksmith. They can talk directly with customers and identify those customer needs that are profitable to serve.

This presents enormous strategic opportunities for many businesses. For example, rather than an insurance company being configured to sell insurance, it might decide that it is better to serve the financial requirements of its most profitable customers. It could offer banking, broking, pension, insurance and mortgage services to core customers. Likewise, rather than the pharmacy being simply a retailer of drugs, it could manage the ongoing health of its customers. Through automatic diagnostics, regular health checks and linkages with the doctor and insurer it could manage the health of a customer over their whole life span. In a different sphere, a company which provides photocopying for small businesses might be able to offer a wider selection of services including management of the communications, presentations, professional services and temporary staff on behalf of core customers. Meanwhile a magazine publisher might set about extracting more value from its readers. If it publishes a golf magazine it could sell green fees, golf videos and merchandise which is tailored to the readers' needs. This would be a major strategic repositioning for the publisher. Rather than launching another title it could invest effort in developing new services for core readers thereby taking a larger share of their pocket.

In each of these cases the supplier would be exploiting the value of its customer base expertise rather than being merely dependent on its product and market expertise. The supplier might not require global economies of scale or leading-edge technology if the supplier can genuinely respond more effectively to the customer's needs/wants than a product-focused competitor. After all, an accounting system which is tailor-made to a customer's needs but uses technology that is two years out of date is often more effective than the latest technology which is purchased 'off the shelf'. The realignment of a business to focus on customer profit opportunities will be a major strategy shift. Rather than being set up to sell products, a supplier might need to be reconfigured to manage the needs/wants of certain profitable customers. The role of sales, product management, production and R&D will need to be rethought so that they can respond quickly, effectively and profitably to specific customer opportunities.

This new era presents enormous strategic opportunities for manufacturers and retailers alike. They can identify the customers which are profitable to serve, and sell them services which are profitable to produce. They might need to ally with other firms in order to satisfy the customer requirements but they would have the opportunity to constantly refine their customer expertise. Of course, many suppliers will find it more profitable to stick to being product experts. But even these firms will have to customize their service to the needs of the customers/customer groups.

However, if a firm is currently failing to manage its customer base, it will not be in a position to exploit the profit opportunities presented in this new business era. Instead it will find that a smarter operator has already poached its best customers.

SUMMARY

■ **The gap between profitable and unprofitable customers is widening because:**

- customers are spoilt for choice, are more sophisticated and find it easier to switch supplier than their predecessors;

- margin pressure is intensifying;

- big customers tend to be getting bigger;

- customer requirements are becoming much more diffused;

- the real costs of serving customers tend to be increasing as a proportion of the suppliers cost base;

- trade channel management is becoming more complex.

■ **A significant proportion of customers can be unprofitable and have no opportunity of becoming profitable. Meanwhile, suppliers are increasingly dependent upon a relatively small group of core profit accounts (note – big customers are not necessarily core profit accounts)**

- a supplier can waste scarce resources by over-serving unprofitable customers whilst under-serving core profit accounts.

- smart competitors can target the core profit customers, thereby torpedoing a suppliers profitability.

▨ **Few companies measure customer profitability**

- sales departments tend to consider sales and gross margins achieved.

- finance departments tend to measure the profitability of divisions and products.

- very few organizations consider the lifetime value of a customer or its Discounted Customer Profitability.

▨ **To improve the management of the customer base a supplier should refine its co-ordination of sales, service, marketing and finance divisions. This can be achieved by formulating a customer base strategy which involves seven stages:**

- determine the value of customers. Identify which customers/trade channels are unprofitable and which produce the majority of profits;

- lock in and develop the core profit accounts;

- explore the routes to increase income;

- reduce the costs of interfacing with customers;

- harness the technology which is available to improve service and reduce the cost of serving customers;

- fix the unprofitable accounts;

- refine the management of the customer lifestages.

▨ **To lock in and develop core profit accounts the supplier needs to:**

- target to achieve and surpass the expectations of profitable customers;

- elevate the relationship with these accounts to become a preferred supplier or partner;

- bond the customer to the supplier organization by developing strong, multifaceted linkages;

- position to service the future needs and wants of these customer groups;

- identify profitable customers which are in decline and target to defend the business;

- increase customer loyalty;

- never take a core profit customer for granted or believe that it is safe.

To increase the income generated from the customer base the supplier should formally explore all the avenues to build sales and raise margins:

- by optimizing the share of pocket, increasing the frequency of purchase and building average transaction values, suppliers can sell more to existing customers;

- new products and services can be developed for the existing customer base. This might be done in partnership with another supplier which has the product and service required, but lacks the knowledge of the customer that is possessed by your organization;

- attract new, profitable customers. Has your organization managed to target the most profitable customers within the market-place or are you dealing with the rump? Benchmark customers versus the competition and if appropriate, construct a focused recruitment strategy to secure the most profitable customers;

- reconsider and possibly overhaul pricing and terms structures. Price lists and trade terms might be outdated and fail to extract the optimal value for the product/service.

Reduce the costs of interfacing with the customers

- review whether it is cost effective to deal directly with a customer or whether it is better to use an intermediary.

- are the right services being performed for the right customer, in the right place at the right time by the most cost effective resource? Organizations often fail to address these issues leaving duplication and inefficiency at the front-line.

- suppliers need to radically streamline the way they interface with customers whilst delivering better service.

The revolution in information and communication systems means that every CEO should be questioning how he/she can harness the new technology to improve the management of the customer base

- new systems allow the size of customer bases to increase. A supplier can centrally process the details for millions of customers at a relatively low cost. Detailed information can be retrieved and interrogated quickly to develop an intimate understanding of customer behaviour and to identify specific profit opportunities.

- communication costs are falling which allow suppliers to interact more quickly and effectively

- computer driven expert systems allow service functions to be automated and improved.

- firms which utilize the new technology will offer superior customer service whilst operating a more controlled, consistent and cost effective front-line.

Suppliers will need to refine their management of each stage in the customer life cycle to raise overall profits. This will be achieved by:

- focusing and formalizing the recruitment of new customers;

- refining the account development;

- slowing down customer attrition.

Business is entering an era where technology and new methods of working will allow suppliers to re-invent the way they work with customers. Acute suppliers will exploit their customer base expertise to develop new products and services. However, if a firm is currently under managing its customer base, it will not be able to exploit the new opportunities, because its best customers will have been poached by a smarter, focused competitor.

NOTES

THE CUSTOMER BASE 'PROFIT GAP' IS WIDENING

Supplier base rationalization

Basu, Sujit Kumar (1993) 'Vendor base reduction', *Purchasing and Supply Management*, June.

Margin pressure

Kelly, Kevin, Schiller, Zachary and Treece, James (1993) 'Cut costs or else', *Business Week*, 22 March.

Partnership

Carter, Tony (1992) 'You get the suppliers you deserve', *Purchasing and Supply Management*, June.

Buyer sophistication

Cammish, Robin and Keogh, Mark (1992) 'A strategic role for purchasing', *Procurement Weekly*, July.
Cayer, Shirley and Morgan, James (1991) 'What it takes to make world class suppliers', *Purchasing*, 15 August.
Millen Porter, Anne (1991) 'Jitt II is here', *Purchasing*, 12 September.

Minahan, Tim (1992) 'Big buyer keeps eye on suppliers', *Purchasing*, 16 January.

Growth of private label

Euromonitor (1995) 'Private label in North America', September.
AC Nielsen, *Homescan* (Year to October 1997).

Changing role of salesforce

Abberton Associates (1993 and 1997) 'Balancing the salesforce equation', *CPM*, July.
Dorsey, David (1994) *The Force*, Random House, Vauxhall.
Fierman, Jaclyn (1994) 'The death and rebirth of the salesman', *Fortune*, 25 July.
America's best salesforces, Sales and Marketing Management, (1997).

LOCK IN CORE PROFIT CUSTOMERS

Loss of loyal customers

Jones, Thomas O and Sasser, W Earl, Jr (1995) 'Why satisfied customers defect', *Harvard Business Review*, November.

Loyalty schemes

Jones, Charles and O'Brien, Louise (1995) 'Do rewards really create loyalty?', *Harvard Business Review*, May.
Miles, Louella(1995) 'Customer Loyalty', *Marketing Guide*, 27 July.
Wilt, Jackie (1995) 'Cold war of loyalty cards', *Retail Week*, 23 October.

Partnership

Everett, Martin (1993) 'Why partners sometimes part', *Sales and Marketing Management*, April.

Morita, Akio (1992) 'Partnering for competitiveness: the role of Japanese business', *Harvard Business Review*, May-June.

Naim, Mohammed and Towill, Denis, Professor (1993) 'Partnership sourcing smoothes supply chain dynamics', *Purchasing and Supply Management*, July.

Sonnenberg, Frank K (1992) 'Partnering, entering the age of co'operation', *Journal of Business Strategy*, September.

Wilson, Larry (1994) *Stop Selling, Start Partnering*, Omneo, USA.

Service and selling

Sewell, Carl (1990) *Customers for Life*, Pocket Books, USA.

Customer retention

Peppers, Don, Pine, Joseph, II and Rogers, Martha (1995) 'Do you want to keep customers forever?', *Harvard Business Review*, March-April.

Jones, T and Sasser, W, 'Why satisfied customers defect', *Harvard Business Review*, November 1995.

INCREASE INCOME

Harnessing intelligence

McKenna, Regis (1995) 'Real-time marketing', *Harvard Business Review*, July-August.

Growth of Far East

Courtis, K S, Chief Economist for Asia Pacific, Deutsche Bank, 'Keynote at the 1994 Pacific Rim Forum'.

Review new markets

Hamilton Frazer, Ian (1995) 'Profile of European Telecom', *Financial Times*, 24 October.

Customer service

Case, John (1991) 'Customer Service: the last word', *Inc. Magazine*, April.

de Jong, Jennifer (1995) 'Turbocharging customer service', *Inc. Technology*, No 2.

Marshall, Sir Colin and Prokesch, Steven E (1995) 'Competing on customer service: an interview with British Airways', *Harvard Business Review*, November-December.

Segmentation

Ehrlich, Evelyn and Wood, Marion B (1991) 'Segmentation: five steps to more effective business-to-business marketing', *Sales and Marketing Management*, April.

Supply chain

Billington, Corcy and Lee, Hau L (1992) 'Managing supply chain inventory: pitfalls and opportunities', *Sloan Management Review*, spring.

Margin improvement

Simon, Hermann (1992) 'Pricing opportunities and how to exploit them', *Sloan Management Review*, winter.

Team selling

Cespedes, F V, Doyle, S X and Freedman, R J (1989) 'Teamwork for today's selling', *Harvard Business Review*, March.

Hyatt Hills, Cathy (1992) 'Making the team', *Sales and Marketing Management*, February.

Murray, Tom (1991) 'Team selling, what's the incentive?', *Sales and Marketing Management*, June.

REDUCE THE COSTS OF INTERFACING WITH CUSTOMERS

Trade channels

Cespedes, Frank V and Corey, E Raymond (1990) 'Managing multiple channels', *Business Horizons*, July.

Profile of RCA

Magrath, A J (1992) 'The gatekeepers', *Across the Board*, April.

IBM software

Sager, Ira (1994) 'The few, the true, the blue', *Business Week*, 30 May.

HARNESS THE TECHNOLOGY

Database management

'The databases of the argument' (1994), *Marketing Week*, 18 November.
Unisys Customer Loyalty (1994) 'Cards win on points', *Marketing Week*, 25 March.
Peppers, D and Rogers, M 'Do you want to keep customers forever', *Harvard Business Review*, April 1992.

New operations

Schiller, Z and Zellner, W (1994) 'Making the middleman an endangered species', *Business Week*, 6 June.

EDI Internet

Freedman, David (1992) 'Retailing in real time (a profile of Wal'Marts EDI systems)', *CIO Magazine*.

Net.gain, Global Business online, *Financial Times Guide*, May 1998.

MAKING IT HAPPEN

Co-ordination of front-line

Cespedes, F V (1995) 'Concurrent marketing, integrating product, sales and service', *Harvard Business School Press*, March.

PREPARE FOR THE NEW ERA

The one to one future

Peppers, Don and Rogers, Martha, PhD (1993) 'The one to one future', *Currency Doubleday*.

Seeing the future first

Hamel, Gary and Prahalad, C K (1994) 'Competing for the future', *Harvard Business School Press*.

Mass customization

Pine, Joseph, II (1993) 'The new frontier in business competition', *Harvard Business School Press*.
Feitzinger, Edward and Lee, Han, 'Mass customization at Hewlett Packard: The Power of Postponement', *Harvard Business Review*, January 1997.

INDEX